D1144537

**Kirklees
Metropolitan
Council** **BATLEY**

Headqu...s:
Pri... ...lexandra Walk
...01 2SU
Libraries and Museums S... ...356

BIRST... 81 17. ...

-7 ° S
10 2 ...

01. FEB 82 0... NOV ...S(AIR) ⇒ MAR

0... CIRSTALL

0... MAR 82 28. DEC 83 30. MAY 1984
  04. JAN 84 21. JUN 84
18. 32 13. MAR 84 15. SEP 84
30. 20. DEC 84
. JUN 82 0. MAR 84 02. MAY 85
17. JUN 82 30 MAY 85A
06 JUL 82 09. APR 34 07. OCT 85

B   227   394   602

PARRY

This book should be returned to the library from which it was borrowed on or before the latest date stamped above.

If not required by another borrower, the loan period may be extended for a further three weeks by post, telephone or personal visit. No more than three renewals permitted. Please quote the nine figure number above the bar code.

TRANS-PENNINE HERITAGE

Reddyshore Scoutgate pack-horse road

TRANS-PENNINE HERITAGE
Hills, People and Transport

KEITH PARRY

WITHDRAWN

PAID FOR REC. NO.

KIRKLEES LIBRARIES & MUSEUMS SERVICE

DAVID & CHARLES
Newton Abbot   London   North Pomfret (Vt)

KIRKLEES LIBRARIES & MUSEUMS

ACC. No. 227 394 602

CLASS 380.509 428

DEPT.	CHECKED
B	H·T

British Library Cataloguing in Publication Data

Parry, Keith
    Trans-Pennine heritage.
    1. Pennine Chain – Description and travel
    I. Title
    914.25′1104857   DA670.P4

    ISBN 0–7153–8019–2

Library of Congress Catalog Card Number 80–68691

Text and sketches © Keith Parry 1981
All rights reserved. No part of this
publication may be reproduced, stored
in a retrieval system, or transmitted,
in any form or by any means, electronic,
mechanical, photocopying, recording or
otherwise, without the prior permission
of David & Charles (Publishers) Limited

Photoset and printed in Great Britain
by Redwood Burn Limited, Trowbridge and Esher
for David & Charles (Publishers) Limited
Brunel House Newton Abbot Devon

Published in the United States of America
by David & Charles Inc
North Pomfret Vermont 05053 USA

CONTENTS

I was born here. I went away and then I came back. I came back, in effect to my homeland. It was a land that had changed, was changing, yet was a land where much remained the same.

Gradually, people are prising the secrets from these hills, piecing together the fragments of a history that is strangely different, oddly complete, peripheral—yet at the very heart of things.

This book is for the people who know and love, or knew and loved, the Pennines, and those others who also search for a hidden heritage.

Keith Parry
Littleborough, Lancashire

January 1980

PROLOGUE:
THE HEART AND MIND
OF THE NORTH

'The North of England' is a familiar enough description, but few people, even people living inside the North, can say precisely where (and, more importantly, *what*) it is.

The Londoner, it is suggested, believes the North begins at Watford Junction; far from believing, the Tynesider would insist the North begins at the Tees. Musically it is the land of *The oak and the ash and the bonny rowan tree*. Meteorologically it is the North—of the United Kingdom.

BBC regional radio insists that the North includes Lincolnshire; the IBA makes Lincolnshire virtually a part of East Anglia. Some Northerners would include Nottinghamshire, others exclude Cheshire.

Heraldically, the North is the land to the north of Trent, coming within the influence of Norroy, King-of-Arms. Inconveniently the Trent flows north for a considerable distance, leaving Lincolnshire in limbo. Local government reorganisation carved up Lincolnshire and made the northern part South Humberside. The same reorganisation split Yorkshire asunder and carved out Greater Manchester and Merseyside from Lancashire and Cheshire. Warrington, once the most decidedly Lancastrian town, was sandwiched between the two new Metropolitan counties and was 'Cestrianised'.

Historically, the North was a separate place—the Danelaw, where the Kings had their courts at Jorvik, the present-day York. This part of England saw a multiplicity of invasions and settlements by Dane and Viking and it was here that their influence was strongest. Scandinavian place-names still predominate in many areas and Scandinavian words pepper Northern speech even today. Later, the North gave its two counties to the Wars of the Roses and felt the impact of the last great invasion by the Scots. Families settled in the North today can trace their ancestry to followers of Bonnie Prince Charlie who fell out of the defeated columns trekking back after the '45.

As early as the fourteenth century, the North of England, although accepted as being 'English', was branded as a separate place, 'apart' from the rest of the country, and only slightly less alien than the 'aliens'—meaning the Scots. Ranulph Higden's *Polychronicon* insists:

> ... Alle the languages of the Northumbres and specially at York is so sharp slyting frotyng and unshape that we sothern men may unneth understande that language.
>
> I suppose the cause be that they be nygh to the alyens that speke strangely.
>
> And also by cause that the kynges of England abyde and dwelle more in the south countrey than in the north countrey.
>
> The cause why they abide more in the south countrey than in the north countrey is by cause that ther is better corn londe more peple more noble cytees and more proufytable havens in the south countrey than in the north.

Understandably, Ranulph Higden could not comprehend the desert-like fastnesses of the North as part of the medieval world. Even so, it had its great monasteries—some of them the greatest—and the rudiments of its trading heritage.

It was not until well on into the eighteenth century that the North began to develop; given its resources in basic terms and its resourcefulness in using them, it is hardly surprising that it developed in the way it did. It was still remote—in land terms at least—from London but the historic cross-country links existed and were already important; even in the seventeenth century the clothiers of Rochdale had petitioned for a navigation to take their goods across country to the important East Coast ports—a primary export route from the North.

Slowly at first, but accelerating, expanding and diversifying, the North built the North, creating not only the industrial system but a social order that was particular to its requirements. By 1900 it was the industrial heartland of the United Kingdom—affluent, thrusting, radical and as 'different' as at any time in its history. Its social order bore little relationship to the traditional English pattern; it was a hierarchy built on money and acumen rather than on precedence. It built, not Jerusalem in

England's green and pleasant land, but a vast trading empire that spanned the world.

It is said, not without justification, that the Northerner feels more at home in North America than he does in Southern England. The historic parallels are there and even today, for all our countrywide supermarkets, plasticated consumerism and networked programming, the North remains surprisingly separate. It is this 'atmospheric' separateness that makes the North what it is and, significantly, the Northerner, going South, finds he has to think before he acts. Coming North, the Southerner, even more significantly, finds his senses disorientated and undergoes a decided culture-shock.

The industrial revolution that framed and formed the North had its counterparts elsewhere. It began in other places long before it struck the North; Ironbridge was in decline by the time the North completed its final cross-Pennine canal and there were parallel industrial ages in Scotland, Wales and even parts of Somerset.

But in the North there were greater (or rather broader) opportunities and, particularly in Lancashire and Yorkshire, the whole 'brew' is stronger. Alongside its mills and mines, its railways and canals, the North built its own special history and that special history has dominated the lives of the Northern people (and there *is* a special Northern people) more completely than most histories have dominated most people. Rediscovering it and evaluating it can be a stimulating, yet unnerving, experience.

Northern history—more specifically the Northern heritage—stretches back something like 250 years and embraces the lives of some 15 million people. Their lines of communication run across country as opposed to radially from London and they feel an affinity with each other rather than with the people living remote from those east-west links. Geographically, their land is divided by the Pennines—the backbone not only of their country, but of the whole of England. At one and the same time the Pennines are watershed, barrier, boundary and symbolic heart. The Pennine rains are not partisan; they fill the Irish and North Seas with equal facility! All the North's roads, railways and canals wishing to link the

9

seas must cross that barrier—rise over it, burrow beneath it or squeeze through the few gaps that exist between the Peak and the Cheviots, a distance of virtually two hundred miles. And the Pennines separating Lancashire from West Yorkshire (more correctly called the South Pennines) are as formidable a barrier as any anywhere.

A physical map shows them to be not particularly high but running virtually unbroken from the Peak to the Aire Gap and throwing out a sizeable spur three quarters of the way across Lancashire. To either side are the industrial conurbations of the West Riding and Lancashire, and the spur of the Rossendale Fells further subdivides the northern and southern parts of Lancashire. Geologically, the map shows them as a mass of gritstone thrusting up between the coal-measures to either side, topped and tailed by the limestone to the north and south and well inside the limits of glaciation. A population map shows a sudden blank between the solid masses of Lancashire and Yorkshire and even a simple road map delineates a markedly sparse area sandwiched between the complicated networks to east and west.

These cross-Pennine roads seem to run to a constant pattern. They finger up the valleys that pierce the gentler Yorkshire slopes, run remarkably straight across the face of the moor, then inch and 'kink' their way down the sharper western side of the hills.

Less manoeuvrable than the roads, the railways and canals burrow under the hills in a series of mighty tunnels—Woodhead and Standedge (and for that matter the tunnel between Bolton and Blackburn)—and even the railway between Manchester and Halifax, allegedly using the low-level Calderdale, is forced into a lengthy tunnel between Littleborough and Todmorden.

It is here, in the area bounded by Calderdale, the M62 and Standedge, the Summit Pass and Cliviger Gorge, Halifax and the Colne valley, that one can trace the development of all the forms of trans-Pennine communication; the transport routes tie together a heritage that is unique.

In a bare handful of miles there are hill tracks, a Roman road, a complex network of pack-horse routes, their single line of stones striding away across the face of the moor; later turnpike roads, some with their toll-houses still intact, the first trans-Pennine

10

canal and railway, the Pennine Way and the Trans-Pennine Motorway, in itself the newest and most remarkable crossing of them all.

Everywhere, the Pennines dominate—cloud-capped or glowing with autumn bracken, delicate under a scattering of snow or black against a threatening sky, they are always there. They gave stone and water and sheep and now give recreation and reservoirs. They framed not only the landscape but the way of life and they remain the dominant feature in the mind's eye as well as on the skyline.

1
'A MOST DISMAL HIGH PRECIPICE'

Taking the Todmorden and Bradford train from Manchester you are aware of the Pennines almost immediately; the main bulk, separating Lancashire from Yorkshire, forms the eastern skyline and on the other side the equally formidable Lancashire spur sweeps in from the west. At Rochdale they are very apparent, circling the town to the north and east, and by the time the train reaches Littleborough they have drawn in to form the two sides of the Roch valley with a seemingly unbroken barrier of hills ahead.

The line crosses the Blackstonedge road, then curves on up the valley, the Todmorden road to the left, the canal to the right and the hills pressing closer. Summit tunnel comes almost without warning—a short, stone-banked cutting, a bridge, a shorter, rocky-sided one and a sudden blackness.

The train emerges to a totally different scene—a narrow, twisting valley of rocky crags, enveloping trees, isolated farmsteads and short Victorian terraces clinging to the precipitous hillside. Road and canal are still there, but turning and twisting within the confining hills.

Todmorden stands where the Cliviger Gorge comes in from the north-west and road, rail and canal turn sharply to the east into Calderdale proper. Todmorden and Hebden Bridge and Mytholmroyd further down the valley fill the few flat acres in the valley bottom and then fling their houses up on to the steep hillsides. Sowerby Bridge, well into Yorkshire, clings to a series of ledges in the steep valley sides and Halifax climbs 700ft from the station at the bottom of the town. Between here and Bradford there are more tunnels and cuttings and viaducts and high embankments before the train finally frees itself of the Pennines.

The Blackstonedge road takes a more direct line from Littleborough to Halifax, climbing tortuously out of the valley with a spectacular rearward view over the spreading Lancashire plain. Before the coming of the M62 Motorway, this was one of the

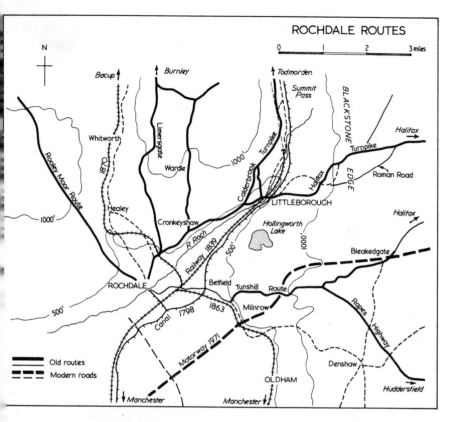

ROCHDALE ROUTES

primary trans-Pennine routes—part of the A58 that linked Merseyside through Bolton and Rochdale with Halifax, Leeds and the A1. Until the coming of the motorway the lorries would grind their way nose to tail, hour after hour up the long, twisting gradient that drew them 800ft up out of the valley to the flat moor top.

To appreciate Blackstonedge and its challenge, one need only travel the old main road from Rochdale. The road drops slightly towards the centre of Littleborough, so the hills are seen fully, rearing up suddenly and solidly. Even Celia Fiennes, sister of Viscount Saye and Sele and an intrepid traveller, was somewhat in awe when she crossed Blackstonedge (and by way of the easier Yorkshire slope) in 1698. She wrote:

Then I came to Blackstonedge, noted all over England for a dismal

13

high precipice and steep in the ascent and descent on Either End; its very moorish ground all about and Even just at the top, tho' so high, that you travel on a Causey wch is very troublesome as its a moist ground soe as is usual on these high hills; they stagnate the air and hold mist and rains almost perpetually.

'Almost perpetually' is something of an overstatement, but it is true that the trans-Pennine traveller will find himself experiencing hill fog (in reality low cloud) on the moor top a hundred days a year on average. To guard against the problems likely to be caused by this phenomenon, the motorway engineers carved a massive cutting to keep the M62 below the 1,300ft level and—hopefully—clear of the cloud.

Defoe's Journey

Daniel Defoe crossed Blackstonedge, from the Lancashire side, in the summer of 1724. His description of the experience is a fascinating one:

Here [Rochdale] for our greater encouragement, though we were but at the middle of August and in some places the harvest hardly gathered in, we saw the mountains covered in snow, and felt the cold very acute and piercing; but even here we found, so in all these northern counties is the case, the people had an extraordinary way of mixing the warm with the cold very happily together; for the store of good ale which flows plentifully in the most mountainous parts of this country seems abundantly to make up for all the inclemencies of the season or difficulties of travelling, adding also the plenty of coals for firing, which these hills are full of.

We mounted the hills, fortified with the same precaution, early in the morning, and though the snow which had fallen in the night lay a little on the ground, yet we thought it was not much; and the morning being calm and clear, we had no apprehension of an uneasy passage, neither did the people at Rochdale, who kindly directed us the way, and even offered to guide us over the first mountains, apprehend any difficulty for us; so we complimented ourselves out of their assistance, which we afterwards very much wanted.

It is not easy to express the consternation we were in when we came near the top of the mountain; the wind blew exceedingly hard, and blew the snow so directly in our faces, and that so thick, that it was impossible to keep our eyes open to see our way. The ground also was so covered in snow, that we could see no track, or when we were in the way or when out; except we were showed it by a fearful precipice on one hand and uneven ground on the other.

In the middle of this difficulty, and as we began to call on one another to turn back again, not knowing what dangers might still be before us, came a surprising clap of thunder, the first that ever I heard in a storm of snow, or, I believe, ever shall; nor did we perceive any lightning to precede the thunder as must naturally be the case; but we supposed the thick falling of snow must prevent our sight . . .

Upon this we made a full stop, and coming all together, for we were three in company, with two servants, we began to talk seriously of going back again to Rochdale, but just then one of our men called out to us and said he was upon the top of the hill and could see over into Yorkshire, and that there was a plain way down on the other side.

Defoe's description is a highly 'atmospheric' one which will strike a chord of memory for many a present-day trans-Pennine traveller. Sudden blizzards (mercifully few in August these days!) can sweep across the moor with alarming and unheralded speed, obliterating the unfenced road within minutes and producing a totally disorientating 'white-out' of Arctic intensity.

Defoe's Route

The description of the journey over Blackstonedge in that snow-swept August, although graphic, is decidedly lacking in physical detail. One theory suggests that he used the old Roman road (which was certainly marked on maps of the time), but there is no precipice, 'fearful' or otherwise, associated with this route until it is over the crest and on the Yorkshire descent. A more generally accepted theory is that Defoe used one of the tracks which was later developed as the coach road. This most certainly has a considerable precipice on one (the western) side, and uneven ground on the other—more correctly the rising slope of the main ridge.

Significantly, Defoe does not mention any settlement after the travellers left Rochdale. Littleborough, although small, was at least 'remarkable' by being the last inhabited place before the mounting of the hills. It is curious that he does not mention a church and cluster of cottages by the river crossing, the half

Robin Hood's Bed, Blackstonedge. Robin Hood's connections with Nottingham were tenuous. He was certainly a Yorkshireman and as the Forest of Sherwood once covered the Pennines hereabouts it is assumed the name is accurate. There are also Robin Hood Rocks at Cragg Vale

dozen larger houses or the prominent old house at Windybank immediately before the climb to the top of Blackstonedge.

This lack of information leads to an entirely new alternative theory: that Defoe did not use the Blackstonedge crossing from Littleborough at all, but the pack-horse route along the Tunshill ridge to the south of the present Hollingworth Lake to reach the crest of Blackstonedge at Bleakedgate. This route would take him clear of Littleborough and the junction there which would have shown the easier route into Yorkshire via the Reddyshore Scoutgate and the Calder valley. Had he used—or intended to use—the Littleborough route, the locals he talked to would surely have suggested to him that there was an alternative route once he reached the village further up the valley.

The Tunshill and Bleakedgate route offers no such alternative. Admittedly, the hamlet of Butterworth, which became Milnrow, would be on his route, but this would seem closer to his starting point and less remarkable as a settlement than Littleborough is. Once the travellers had left Butterworth they would be high on the ridge with the hamlet left quickly behind.

Defoe mentions, albeit in passing, the coal that was abundant in the area. Coal was mined (more specifically dug out of the hillside) in hundreds of places around Rochdale, but the workings at Butterworth were particularly noteworthy and developed into a colliery which was operational until relatively recently. Defoe's casually descriptive remark may have been sparked off by something he heard in conversation in Rochdale when the proposed journey was being discussed, something on the lines of 'by way of the coal workings at Butterworth'.

The Tunshill pack-horse track runs along the crest of the ridge reaching out westwards from the main bulk of Blackstonedge. The ridge falls sharply to Longdenend Clough, which could be the 'fearful precipice' he describes. The uneven ground on the other side could refer to the saw tooth of hills on the crest of the ridge.

Where the ridge joins the main bulk of Blackstonedge there is a half mile or so of level ground before the land begins to fall towards Yorkshire (the actual 'crest' is much sharper than further north) and this could be the point where the despairing travellers totally lost the way. It seems to have been only a short time before one of the party 'called out to us and said he was upon the top of the hill and could see over into Yorkshire'; on the route by way of Littleborough it would have been a considerable time, and hours if they had diverged even slightly from the accepted route.

Most significant of all, Defoe does not mention the Roman road or the existence of a broad paved way, which suggests he had no knowledge of its existence. Celia Fiennes, on the other hand, does at least mention 'a Causey' at the top of Blackstonedge—information that could hardly have slipped from the minds of the local people in the quarter century between her journey and Defoe's.

So the theory now is that the two travellers used entirely separate routes, both starting and ending in Rochdale and Halifax, both crossing Blackstonedge, but one to the north, the other to the south of the main peak of Robin Hood's Bed.

2
ROMAN, 'ROMAN' or . . . ?

Even though the existence of a Roman road over Blackstonedge was accepted as fact before and during Daniel Defoe's time, its origins were subsequently challenged and became the subject of heated controversy. Richard James, who wrote his *Iter Lancastrense* in 1636, declared positively:

> Ashton of Middleton, to ye I went
> . . . and some miles beyond thy home,
> Mounted upon thy horse we did roam,
> Under thy guidance to a Roman waye,
> High cast yet standing as perchance it laye
> From Yorck to Chester . . .

The facts are there, concealed under the poetry; James was shown the random remains of a road high on the moors some distance from Ashton's home in Middleton.

The Blackstonedge crossing was fortified during the Civil War (as was the Bleakedgate route to the south) by Colonel Rosworm; it is generally accepted that it was the Roman road that was so guarded and some of the construction works on the crest are attributed to this time. Celia Fiennes refers to the causeway at the end of that century and Sayers' map, published in 1728, four years after Defoe's crossing, indicates that it was a Roman road extending from Manchester to Aldbrough in Yorkshire.

A few years later, however, the Reverend John Watson writes, 'Having searched the country hereabouts with infinite labour I never could make the least discovery of any such thing as a Roman road over Blackstonedge.' But Watson was one of the opponents of the Roman theory.

In 1765 in his *Roman Lancashire* Thomas Watkins observed, 'The most singular fact connected with this road is that no-one has ever seen or heard of any portion of it between Manchester and Blackstonedge.' He and many others tended to dismiss the 'Roman' theory more or less on balance of probabilities.

The arguments reached a peak in the late nineteenth century and echoes of it, like the reverberations of Defoe's clap of thunder, have rumbled on into the recent past. Nowadays the road is generally accepted as being Roman, if only by default. The argument is: 'If it isn't Roman, what is it?' For a dozen centuries after the Romans left, roads were a rarity and certainly roads in the Pennine area and a structure of this complexity was unheard of. And unnecessary Journeys such as those of Celia Fiennes and Daniel Defoe were considered remarkable enough to be written about and the primitive pack-horse tracks—like those along the rim of the Summit Pass and Calderdale—were sufficient for the needs of the sparsely inhabited country in the Pennines. The technology needed to build a road of the dimensions of the Roman road over Blackstonedge was not developed until the time when such a massive construction would have been recorded. There is no such documentation; nor is there any mention of any exploit of such a nature in local folk-lore.

The road certainly features in local history. It was known to the inhabitants on the Yorkshire slopes as 'the Danes' Road', at least suggesting that a definite route existed which was associated with that period of history. The route would seem a logical one, reaching westwards from the Ouse towards Blackstonedge and Manchester. There is ample evidence of Danish settlement in the Pennine highlands and a curious enclave around the banks of the Mersey in the Manchester area. It has been suggested that the Danes who settled around Davyhulme and Flixton reached the Mersey either from the sea or by way of the old Roman road from the Peak District of Derbyshire. Equally, they could have used a Roman route over Blackstonedge.

Research in the 1920s suggested the remains of a Roman road at Moston in suburban Manchester and a line running north-east near Milnrow; furthermore, there is a 'Roman Road' in Royton and the very recent excavations in Manchester tend to reinforce the argument for the Roman road over Blackstonedge. It is now being suggested that Mancunium was one of the major manufacturing towns of Roman Britain and in this case it would be logical to suggest that the road pattern could be far more complex than previously imagined.

Over the centuries there has been a persistent rumour of a

Roman camp associated with the section of road in the Black-stonedge area and, currently, archaeologists assert that they are fully aware of the site but insist that the actual whereabouts must remain a closely guarded secret to avoid the depredations of the ever-present metal detectors. Undeterred, a local enthusiast began digging near the road in the summer of 1979 and received considerable publicity regarding the large hole he had made in the moor and the artifacts he had discovered. He was speedily informed by the Steward to the Lord of the Manor (whom few people, presumably, knew existed) that the moorland was under his jurisdiction and such digging unauthorised and unwelcome! 'Establishment' archaeologists viewed the excavated material and pronounced it of interest and suggested it dated from some time between Roman times and the early twentieth century! The general consensus was that it was probably associated with the extensive quarrying which took place near the road during the various building booms of the nineteenth century.

Theories

The existence of two Roman camps in the Pennines, but to the south of Blackstonedge, tends to cloud the case for the location of a third. Castleshaw is near Delph and above the Tame valley; Melandra was a substantial settlement over the hill from there, and Herbert C. Collins, writing in the late 1940s, favours a more southerly route—Melandra to Castleshaw, north by way of the Readycon Gap and Bleakedgate and heading for Colne. He further suggests a cross-Pennine route by way of the Tunshill ridge and Bleakedgate. He suggests that this road is well engin-eered and has its gradients eased by digging into the hillside at various points, an unusual feature in purely pack-horse roads. However, this 'easing' is precisely what happened when—for instance—the old Reddyshore Scoutgate was improved to take wheeled traffic. Furthermore, if the present-day theory about Defoe's route is correct, the case for a Roman road along the Tunshill ridge is considerably less firm. He produces one im-portant piece of evidence. The arm of a silver statuette was found in this area; attached to it was a plate inscribed with a dedication to Valerius Rufus of the Sixth Legion. This Sixth Legion came

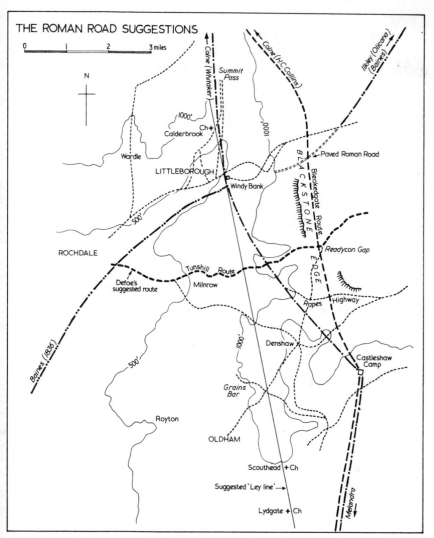

THE ROMAN ROAD SUGGESTIONS

0   1   2   3 miles

N

Colne (Whitaker)

Colne (H C Collins)

Ilkley (Olicana) (Baines)

Summit Pass

1000'

Calderbrook

Ch+

Wardle

LITTLEBOROUGH

Windy Bank

BLACKSTONE

Bleakedgate Route

Paved Roman Road

500'

ROCHDALE

Readycon Gap

EDGE

Tunshill Route

Defoe's suggested route

Milnrow

Rapes Highway

Baines (1836)

500'

1000'

Denshaw

Castleshaw Camp

Grains Bar

Royton

OLDHAM

Scouthead +Ch

Suggested 'Ley line'→

Lydgate +Ch

Melandra

Celia Fiennes	'A causeway', 1698
Daniel Defoe	No mention, 1724
Sayers	'Manchester to Aldborough', 1728
Britannia Romana	Yes, 1732
Watson	No trace, 1735
Warburton	Yes, 1753
Watkins	No trace from Manchester, 1765
Whitaker	Ancoats–Chadderton–Royton, 1775
	(Camps: Colne, Windybank, Castleshaw)
Baines	Castleton–Rochdale–Ilkley, 1836
Collins	Colne–Bleakedgate–Castleshaw, 1940s

to Britain with Hadrian in AD 120, was stationed on the Northumbrian Wall, at York and at Ribchester. There are also traces of the Legion at Manchester and Melandra.

The Roman road (or perhaps roads?) emerges from time to time through history, a continual tantalising enigma that remains to be solved. James mentions it in 1636, Celia Fiennes describes a definite causeway sixty years later. Defoe makes no mention in 1724, Sayers shows it a mere four years later. Watson failed to find it, but *Britannia Romana* published in 1732 says specifically that the road was so much sunk beneath the surface that the author had difficulty in finding it. Warburton's map of 1753 shows it, Thomas Watkins failed to find any mention or trace of its route from Manchester to Blackstonedge in 1765. A mere ten years later, J. Whitaker in his *History of Manchester* describes its route in detail—through Ancoats, via Chadderton and Royton and Baines' *History of Lancashire* in 1836 mentions that a Roman road crossed Castleton in a north-easterly direction and was part of a route from *Rochdale* to *Ilkley*. At the back of the mind is the nagging suspicion created by the recent hypothesis about ancient trackways—'Ley Lines' of immeasurable age—one of which (inconveniently!) is supposed to traverse the Roch valley area from somewhere above Littleborough southeast along the Pennine foothills.

Whitaker pointed out that there was ample evidence of pre-Roman habitation in the Pennines and suggested that these early settlements and communications could have been taken over and impoved by the Romans. He linked together a number of British camps from Colne via Windybank—the prominent house above the valley at Littleborough—to Castleshaw and beyond. This bears out the Ley Line theory, so long as the theory is allowed some deviation in hilly country, but confuses the issue regarding a route via the Readycon Gap.

Much was made, by both pro- and anti-Roman factions, of the method of paving adopted for the road. A line of large stones is laid down the middle of the highway and the 'anti' faction pointed out that these stones are typical of the usual pack-horse road paving stones and suggested they were worn deep by the action of the horses' hooves. Maxim allows himself the indulgence of several novel explanations for the stones. He attributes the wearing of the centre stones to chains and cables used in association with a winding mechanism at the top of the slope, to water, to the draining effect of the stones, to the marching of a single column of soldiers and—most spectacularly—to the transporting of Danish boats over Blackstonedge! To be fair, Maxim does not claim these outlandish theories as his own, preferring to include them merely to weight his argument against the road being Roman.

The anti-Roman faction tended to compare the road favourably with the known examples of pack-horse roads, such as the Reddyshore Scoutgate. This argument ignores the important fact that the Blackstonedge road runs straight up a considerable gradient whereas pack-horse tracks would tend to take an easier route (the Tunshill—Bleakedgate example for instance) and the Blackstonedge road is almost twice as wide as an 'improved' pack-horse road. And certainly the Reddyshore Scoutgate, when it was improved, was widened by the addition of a second line of stones—to take the wheels of carts. It would seem strange that an entirely different solution was used a few miles away at Blackstonedge.

The Evidence Today

A recent brief encounter with the Roman road convinced at least one previously hesitant observer—an officer from the Department of the Environment, who agreed that it had all the ingredients necessary for it to be considered genuine. He had been called in to advise on the erosion occuring along the exposed section on the western slope. This very erosion seems to reduce the strength of one of J. L. Maxim's arguments. (He suggests that it is strange that the paving should have been so little overgrown.) But over the past few years the coarse earth along the sides of the road has been washed away, particularly after a couple of dry summers, and carrying this effect backwards through time it is less surprising that little growth had occurred on the surface. In a handful of years the erosion has reached a point where the paving stands well clear of the surrounding earth and, in some places, is in danger of being undermined.

Nowadays, the arguments also seem to have been eroded away

Roman road, Blackstonedge. The exposed pavement on the western slope—above Littleborough

by the constant washing of more explicit research material. The Roman road is now scheduled as an Ancient Monument and a magnet for visitors. They struggle up the steep slope (very often ignoring the easier route along the Pennine Way) to take in the breathtaking view from the top of the Edge. Some must surely ask themselves why anyone in his right mind would build a cart-track on such a difficult line (approaching one in four) when an easier and lower crossing point was available just to the north. But it *is* possible to envisage the Romans building such a road, given that their civilisation was nothing if not expansive and monumental!

At the top of the Edge where the Roman road breasts the hill stands the Aiggin Stone, and here we enter an entirely new world of fantasy. Given the Roman connection, 'aiggin' could be a corruption of 'agger'—unfortunately a word with a multiplicity of meanings. It can denote a pile or mound, a dike or rampart, even a road (because of the raised nature of such Roman constructions). But the derivation may be something far more mundane. 'Aiggin' may be simply the local pronunciation of 'edging', and the stone is characteristic of those way-markers commonly found on the pack-horse routes. The stone itself is about 7ft high, an irregular block of local gritstone; the only decoration is a simple incised cross and the letters 'I.T.' beneath.

The road changes direction slightly as it starts the descent down the gentler Yorkshire side of Blackstonedge and crosses Black Castle Clough by way of a bridge which is definitely not Roman—it was reconstructed in the flat 'pack-horse' style in the 1930s. A mile or so further on it joins up with the modern Blackstonedge road.

The Roman road over Blackstonedge is yet another enigma, one of the secrets still hidden in the mists of Pennine time. The exposed fragment appears suddenly, 18ft wide, climbing resolutely up the bare face of the moor. It is substantially paved and the larger troughed stones mark out the centre of the highway. Was the trough to take a brushwood 'brake' for descending chariots? Was it filled with turf to give a firm foothold for the horses? Was it a gutter? Was it simply worn away by the passage of horses and men? The fragment disappears again, possibly marked by a frail line on the map along the slope of the moor above Ripponden and again crossing Norland Moor a mile further on across the Ryburn valley.

Did it run from Manchester to York? To Ilkley or to Aldbrough? Was it simply a link-road between *two* roads running up either side of the Pennine ridge? Was the Blackstonedge Roman camp at Windybank? Is it really where the experts say it is, or did the local enthusiast dig up what remained at the foot of Robin Hood's Bed in the summer of 1979? The questions erupt in the minds of the students of this curious road.

Just occasionally, when the visitors have gone and one is alone on the road, there is a hint, a drifting whisper, of the answer to the questions. It hovers in the air, just out of reach, tantalising the questioner. The Sixth Legion knew the answer, but reach for it now and it fades away as surely as a curlew's call.

3
GATES, CROSSES AND CUTS

The basic topography of the South Pennines was finally formed during the Ice Age. The coal-measures (more correctly known as 'Westphalian' today) had been eroded away, exposing a massive spine of the familiar forms of gritstone which the geologists label 'Namurian'. A river ran eastwards roughly on the line of the present Yorkshire Calder.

The Ice Age glaciers covered the areas to the north-west and the Lancashire plain, and the most recent research suggests that a finger of the north-west glacier forced its way down from the Burnley area to reach a point roughly half-way along the upper Calder valley.

With the melting of the glaciers, the Calder valley was gouged deeper by the off-shoot from the north-west and a massive lake built up in the Roch valley. This eventually cut through the ridge to the south of Todmorden and scoured out the Summit Pass between Littleborough and Calderdale. So formed the 'Y' shaped pattern of narrow valleys that were to become so important later.

The valleys have a significant 'shelf' above the river level, the result of erosion as the water carved out the valleys. Nowhere is this more apparent than in the Littleborough area where the melting waters of the glacier carved out sharp, steep-sided cloughs which very nearly look man-made. The shelf along the eastern side of the valley is particularly sharply serrated with the small side-valleys cutting well back into the shelf above the main valley. In Calderdale too the shelf exists and it is quite possible to look across from one side of the valley to the other without seeing the deeper winding cleft in the valley floor which carries road, rail and canal.

Above this shelf rises the high moor with its thick covering of peat and exposed rocky outcrops—the 'Edges'. The South Pennines are not mountains—nowhere do they top 2,000ft, but, formed as they are and being exposed to the vagaries of the weather, they throw together a hard, primitive landscape that has proved a formidable opponent time and time again. The high moor has been inhabited—intermittently. There are traces of Neolithic and Megalithic Man and flints can be picked up on the higher slopes. There are earthworks and barrows and at least one supposed site of a stone circle.

The Pack-horse Tracks

The earliest tracks across the moor were certainly prehistoric and from them developed a complex network of routes running between the valleys. The valleys themselves were to be avoided, being prone to flooding, heavily wooded and virtually uninhabitable.

The settlements were developed along the shelf above the valley and gradually spread to form a chain of small hamlets linked to each other along the shelves. The links formalised into the characteristic pack-horse roads which for generations provided the only means of communication within the area. To either side the plains developed their towns and farms; the people of the Pennines, whether officially Yorkshire or Lancashire men, shared a common landscape and experienced a mutual heritage.

Along the other Pennine valleys, notably in the Rossendale Fells, a similar pattern developed and a complicated series of pack-horse track links emerged, tying the area together. The pack-horse roads rim the valleys, generally staying below the 1,000ft level (to avoid the persistent cloud of the high moor), but descending to the valley floor itself only where absolutely necessary—usually to cross and rise to the opposite shelf.

Other tracks link the valleys across the moorland, fanning out across the flat tableland, heading for the next prominent Edge and the descent to the next valley beyond. Some were to become major trading routes—the Long Causeway, for instance, linking Halifax and Burnley along the northern rim of Calderdale. The Reddyshore Scoutgate links the Long Causeway with Rochdale by way of the heights above the Summit Pass and a series of feeder routes connects this track with the Limersgate track along the eastern side of the Whitworth valley.

Limersgate was, in fact, one of the main roads from Man-

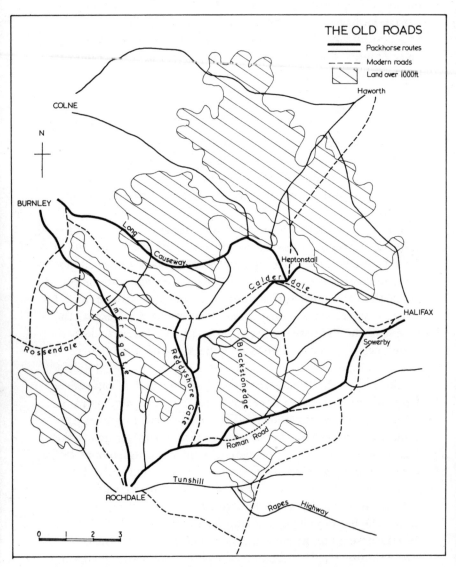

THE OLD ROADS

- Packhorse routes
- Modern roads
- Land over 1000ft

COLNE

N

Haworth

BURNLEY

Long Causeway

Heptonstall

Calderdale

HALIFAX

Limersgate

Reddyshore Gate

Blackstonedge

Sowerby

Rossendale

Roman Road

Tunshill

ROCHDALE

Rapes Highway

0 1 2 3

chester to the north and the Scots under Bonnie Prince Charlie struggled back this way after the incursion of 1745, or so local legend has it. But the '45 is, in Limersgate terms, comparatively recent history. The road takes its name from the trade of transporting limestone, quarried around the Clitheroe area and brought down to sweeten the poor soil of the South Pennines;

some was also used in the iron trade. 'Gate' is a common word hereabouts and simply means 'road' or 'way'.

Limersgate leaves Rochdale for the north by way of Cronkeyshaw. From Cronkeyshaw, it runs along the western slopes of Brown Wardle, a hill with evidence of early settlement and fortification. It climbs, now clear of the Roch valley, by Hades Hill (with the site of a Neolithic barrow on its highest slopes) to run along the ridge between the Whitworth and Summit valleys. It dips to cross the present-day Todmorden–Bacup road at Sharneyford, then rises again, this time to run along the ridge parallel to the Cliviger Gorge. Limersgate is, indeed, literally a highroad; by the time it reaches Hades Hill it is well over 1,300ft above sea-level, having climbed a good 900ft from the centre of Rochdale. At its highest point, on the ridge separating the Whitworth valley and Summit Pass, it is well over 1,400ft up.

To the east of Limersgate, the Reddyshore Scoutgate (which translates as 'the road along the steep red cliffs') runs on a more or less parallel course, this time along the edge of the Summit Pass between Littleborough and Todmorden. This road was part of the important system of pack-horse routes connecting Rochdale to the Long Causeway, Halifax and the Worth valley.

This road originally diverged from the Rochdale–Blackstonedge–Halifax route by the river-crossing at Littleborough. It cut across the fields to Townhouse, a habitation on a very early site, then climbed to the valley-side shelf and Calderbrook. From here it climbed yet again to run along the very edge of the cliff along the western rim of the Summit Pass. At its highest point it is very nearly 1,000ft above sea-level and there is a sheer drop of 300ft to the floor of the valley below. Travelling the Reddyshore Scoutgate in anything but the most clement weather must have been a worrying experience!

A third track ran up through the village of Wardle, then split, the arms joining up with the Limersgate and Reddyshore Scoutgate to either side.

These were busy trade routes, with long lines of sturdy Galloway horses picking their slow way across the moors. Lime came from the north, woollen goods woven locally were carried over the hills to the market at Halifax. Everything which could not be made locally had to be transported in this way.

The pack-horse roads fan out from Rochdale, which is sited strategically at the foot of the Pennines and the Rossendale Fells. One climbs over Rooley Moor north-westwards to Newchurch-in-Rossendale and over to the valley of the Lancashire Calder. Then there are the Limersgate, Wardle and Reddyshore Scoutgate roads, the Blackstonedge route and the track out to the east along the Tunshill ridge. And from this latter route a track—known as the Rapes Highway—diverged to cross the moor to Marsden and the Colne valley.

On the other side of the Pennines was Halifax, another important commercial centre. From here pack-horse roads ran north, north-westwards to Haworth and the Worth valley, and out to the west and the Long Causeway. The Blackstonedge route left by way of Sowerby, the old hand-loom weavers' hamlet above the 'modern' Sowerby Bridge, and here a road branched off to run parallel to the Long Causeway, but this time along the southern rim of the Calder valley.

The Long Causeway

The Long Causeway itself is a trade route of great antiquity, probably based on a Bronze Age track. The roadside crosses which mark the route from Halifax to Burnley have been the subject of much research (and not a little argument) among antiquarians. The mixture of cultures in the South Pennines means that they could be Celtic, Anglian or Norse. Gradually, over the past fifty years, historians have come to the conclusion that at least one, Mount Cross, shows Viking influences. The argument for this is sound; the Vikings began to move east from the Irish Sea coast from about AD 950 and were certainly in Cumbria before this date. They moved gradually across country and settled the high moorland and their place-names litter the South Pennines.

Other tracks linked these main routes. Mount Cross stands on the Long Causeway above the hamlet of Shore, itself high above the Cliviger Gorge. In 1595 a case was heard in the Lancashire Duchy court which involved the rights of way 'for cart and carriage and on foot between Rochdale, Scaitcliffe, Shorey (Shore), Brunley, Clidrawe (Clitheroe) and Colne diverting from the High Street (The Long Causeway) between Brunley and Halifax at or near Shipden (Stiperden), through the land of James Crabtree and through a gate called Lydgate then following the water to Thrutchley Holme and on to Scaitcliffe and Adamhooey and from thence to the town of Rochdale'.

The old trade route along the edge of the Cliviger Gorge and Calderdale was even commemorated in rhyme:

> Brunley for ready money,
> Mereclough nooa trust,
> Yo tekken a peep at Stiperden,
> But ca' at Kebs yo must.
> Blackshaw Yed for travellers,
> An' Heptonstall for trust,
> Hepton Brig for landladies,
> And Midgley in the moor.
> Luddenden's a waarm shop,
> Roylehead's varry cold,
> An' if yo get to Halifax
> Yo mun bi varry bold.

Mereclough, Blackshawhead, Heptonstall, Midgley and Luddenden were all weaving hamlets. Luddenden, tucked deep in its valley, can indeed be warm, particularly when the traveller has endured the rigours of the old road, and Royle Head, even though it is now part of suburban Halifax, is a thousand feet up and can be extremely cold!

At Allerscholes, on the Reddyshore Scoutgate, there is an old mile-post marking an important junction. From here, tracks lead to Rochdale, Todmorden, Burnley and, again, Halifax. The distances are marked on the four sides of the post: 5 to Rochdale; 2 to Todmorden; 9 to Burnley; and 10 to Halifax. The name Allerscholes has been found in records as early as 1475, which gives some indication of the age of this important moorland link.

Weavers and Merchants

Heptonstall, a trustworthy place according to the old rhyme, was an important centre at a very early date. The old church here, dedicated to St Thomas à Becket, was established in 1260, and

31

the Cloth Hall (where hand-woven cloth pieces were brought for sale) was built by the Waterhouse family of Shibden Hall around 1550. Halifax itself had a building known as the Cloth Hall in the seventeenth century but the hall at Heptonstall was not totally superseded until the Piece Hall at Halifax was opened in 1779.

It is not surprising, then, that the whole of the South Pennines looked to Halifax as its major trading centre. As early as 1698 (the year that Celia Fiennes made her perilous way over Blackstonedge) the 'Clothiers of Ratchdale' supported a Parliamentary Bill to improve the Aire Navigation, a vitally important link between the hinterland and the East Coast. In the event it was to be a full hundred years before the building of the canal gave them easy access through the Pennine barrier.

Rochdale had, in fact, a market of its own, and often a local merchant would be in partnership with a like-minded merchant in Manchester or even London. The Lancashire side of the Pennines specialised in the coarser cloths called 'cottons', 'rugs' and 'friezes'. 'Frizing' and 'cottoning' were both finishing processes applied to woollen cloth. Yorkshire handled the finer cloths and in 1588 it was said that, 'The Hallyfaxe Men occupie fyne woole most out of Lincolnshire, and there corse wolle they sell to the men at Ratchdall'. Even a casual remark of this kind indicates the importance of the cross-Pennine links between Halifax and Rochdale.

The spinning and weaving of wool had begun in the moorland farmhouses and there are still a number of old farmsteads showing signs of integral weaving rooms. Then the weaving hamlets grew up along the higher slopes of the valleys, linked by the complex network of trade routes. In its simplest form, the woollen 'industry' consisted of a weaver/farmer spinning the wool from the backs of his own sheep, making cloth sufficient for his own needs first, then disposing of the rest of his production. He would simply roll up the finished cloth, sling it across his shoulders and set off over the moor to sell it in the market at Rochdale or Halifax.

Later, the system expanded and diversified. The weavers collected into settlements—the weaving villages. Merchants acted as middlemen, selling the raw wool to the weaver and buying back the finished cloth, and many a small manor house has its

'Takkin' In Shop' alongside. Whole families worked on the cloth and the many hundreds of characteristic weavers' cottages throughout the area testify to the magnitude of the hand-loom weaving industry.

Weaving (as opposed to spinning) by hand lasted well into the nineteenth century and some villages were active 'factories' long after the coming of the mill system. The hand-loom weaver was a skilled craftsman and fiercely independent. He could work all the daylight hours (often he had to), but he could equally well take a day off if he felt so inclined; it was quite usual to add Monday to the traditional Sabbath rest.

By the 1840s, the hand-loom weavers' craft was a dying industry—the mills had taken over. In his book *Walks in South Lancashire*, Thomas Bamford records a conversation between a gentleman and a calico weaver at Smithy Nook (a group of cottages in the hamlet of Calderbrook, near Littleborough).

Gentleman: And how much may you have for weaving a yard of calico?
Weaver: A yard, Mon? They'n so much a cut.
Gentleman: And how many yards are there in a cut?
Weaver: Why! Theer's thirty yards i'th'Smithy Nook cal'; an' they gettin fro' a shilling to eighteenpence a cut: that at a shilling'll be nowt a yard, will it neaw?

It could take a weaver up to twelve days to set up and weave one 'cut' on a hand loom.

The Villages

The weaving villages have a fascination all their own. Mankinholes sits on its shelf, backed by the sweep of Erringden Moor, high over an invisible Todmorden hidden in the valley below. There are few modern excrescences—everything is part of that pre-industrial isolation once so much a part of this landscape. The water trough is there as are the Tudor and Jacobean gables and the many-mullioned windows of the weaving room.

Quakers lived at Bottomley too, a tiny weaving hamlet in the Walsden valley at the bottom of Salter Gate Rake, the connecting track between the Reddyshore Scoutgate and Mankinholes.

33

Here the residence of one Joshua Fielden was a registered meeting-place in 1689. The name Fielden weaves in and out of the history of Todmorden to the present day. The family were mill-owners, parliamentarians, railway company directors (after being staunch opponents of the plans to build a canal) and benefactors to the town.

Like so many prosperous families throughout the Pennine area, the Fieldens could trace their ancestry back to a man who wove his own cloth and tramped over the hills to sell it in the market at Halifax. When you have a name tied so firmly to an area, history is very close at hand.

Bottomley, Mankinholes, Calderbrook and Heptonstall (and Haworth, Golcar, Mill Bank and a multitude of other places) clung to the edges of the moorland wilderness. They were hives of industry, yet isolated from each other, linked by the pack-horse tracks that reached out along the valley sides and over the hills. The single line of stones would climb away, the strings of 'Gals' make their slow way from village to village, hill-top cross to hill-top cross . . .

More than one modern walker with a name like Fielden or Mitchell or Butterworth has been prompted to delve into his family history after a tramp along these tracks. Very often he finds that his ancestors tramped the same tracks two hundred years ago—and a back-pack must feel very much like a fustian piece when the track is steep and the wind whips across the moor!

4
VOICES THUNDERING IN THE WILDERNESS

Noncomformist religion came early to the South Pennines; within a very short time after the passing of the Toleration Act in 1689 Quaker meeting-houses were registered in Haworth, Mankinholes, Bottomley and Todmorden. By 1704, indeed, the Baptists had taken over the original Society of Friends home in Todmorden as the Quakers had moved on to larger premises.

The uplands provided a fertile ground for the seeds of the new religions and ultimately the roots went deep. The all-embracing character of Nonconformism was peculiarly well-suited to the society—not to mention the topography—of the area and ultimately it became a pervading (some would say dominating) influence. Its philosophies reflected every facet of life and many of the principles persist.

The old parish churches had been medieval establishments controlled by the abbeys, notably Whalley and Stanlawe, and, after the dissolution of the abbeys, by clerics many miles removed from the developing villages high in the Pennines. For a time, for instance, Rochdale came within the jurisdiction of the Bishops of Lichfield!

Halifax probably had a church in Saxon times, but the earliest reliable date is for a Norman church about 1120. Additions to this church were made in 1290, but the main fabric of the present building is fifteenth-century. Heptonstall Old Church was established in 1260; the church at Rochdale is another fifteenth-century one.

Chapels were set up within the enormous medieval parishes. Littleborough chapel, for instance, was erected in 1471 (although a priest had been in residence at Stubley Hall before this date) and the Saddleworth chapelrie was established as early as the thirteenth century. The register of curates at Saddleworth tells a familiar story. From 1215 until the Dissolution they were appointed by the abbeys at Stanlawe and Whalley; after that date by the Vicars of Rochdale until the direct jurisdiction was taken away in 1831.

Although Todmorden had two churches—in the centre of the present town and at Cross Stone—the chain of chapels-of-ease between Rochdale and Halifax (Littleborough, Todmorden, Cross Stone and Heptonstall) were ill-sited for the needs of the area and the inhabitants of the upland settlements had long distances to travel to a place of worship. They had an even longer distance to travel if they wanted to get married; until well into the nineteenth century people from Todmorden, for instance, had to travel all the way to Rochdale to be married.

'Mass' weddings were a feature of this time; a number of couples (legend has it that the record number was thirty-two) assembled at the church and were married in one gigantic ceremonial. The story (hopefully apocryphal) goes that a certain Rochdale vicar concluded the service by announcing, 'Now! You're all wed. You know what to do so get about it!' It is not surprising, therefore, that many couples dispensed with the formalities of a church ceremony. If they wanted to formalise a union they would do so by the simple expedient of joining hands and, witnessed by their friends, jumping over a broom laid on the ground. Hence the term 'livin' over th'brush'! Nowadays that suggests an informal arrangement, but two hundred years ago a common-law marriage was a marriage none the less.

There was an ever-present danger of in-breeding in the isolated moorland settlements and the lack of religious stricture, plus the extremely primitive living conditions, produced some totally illicit relationships. There is a story, regarding the former, that a doctor newly arrived in Smallbridge, between Littleborough and Rochdale, was confronted by his first patient who announced, 'There's nowt wrang wi' me, but Ah've just come to tell thi that we're that inbred reaund here we're all puddled [slightly mad]!' A recent television adaptation of *Wuthering Heights* was roundly condemned by the critics as being too violent, gloomy and 'physical'. The picture of life at the turn of the eighteenth century illustrated by the television director from the words of Emily Brontë was certainly more true-to-life than the glossy Hollywood 'classic' and probably far more accurate than most Pennine folk would care to admit.

The Spread of Nonconformism

Although the population in the South Pennines was expanding throughout the eighteenth and nineteenth centuries, the Established Church stayed in its medieval locations in the towns; it was not until mid-Victorian times that additional churches were built. Meanwhile, Nonconformism pushed outwards and upwards until every settlement, however small and remote, had at least one chapel. It is important to remember, though, that Nonconformism began within the Established Church, and the South Pennines were a hotbed of agitation in the early days of the new religious persuasions. Independents, Quakers and Baptists were active throughout the area in the early 1700s, but it was within the confines of the parish churches (and notably around St Michael's at Haworth) that the convulsions of early Methodism were felt.

The usual pattern obtained at Haworth; a decree dated 1317 commands the rector and vicar of Bradford and the freeholders of Haworth to pay the curate of Haworth the salary due to him in the proportion to which they had been liable from ancient times; so a church existed there at this date. By 1660 the poll tax assessed that the population was 490 and the total rents from land and mills was £1,020.

Grimshaw and Wesley

The sounds of dissension were already being heard around the Worth valley and on 10 October 1689 (immediately after the Act of Toleration) the house of James Smith was registered as a Quaker meeting-house. The home of one Thomas Fethis was registered in 1693 and a third house, that of William Clayton, in 1696. The influence of the itinerant preacher George Fox had been felt strongly in the area and in 1726 the Reverend Isaac Smith, whose father had travelled with Fox, was appointed vicar of Haworth.

Smith Senior had stayed within the Church of England and had been much discriminated against. All the same, he had educated many young men—including his sons—for the ministry. He had been vicar at Mixenden and Warley, just above Halifax, but his unorthodox views meant that he was always in danger of retribution from the Church authorities and the outraged purists of the Church of England. Often he was forced to preach at night and on more than one occasion narrowly escaped capture by the militia who had been called in to suppress him. But by the time he died in 1736, the Dissenters were firmly established in the villages of the South Pennines.

Isaac Smith himself died in 1741 and the following year the Reverend William Grimshaw succeeded to the living. Grimshaw had been the minister of the church of St Mary's, Todmorden, for ten years and was already influenced by the teachings of Benjamin Ingham and the Moravian John Toelshig. Shortly after Grimshaw's arrival in Haworth William Darney ('Scotch Will') visited the area. Grimshaw was impressed, then totally committed, and the stage was set for one of the most monumental religious dramas of all time!

'Phenomenal' is the only word which properly describes William Grimshaw. He preached to vast crowds all over the area, travelling constantly, trudging and riding all over the wild uplands. His message was clear and strong, his charisma messianic. It is reported that on one occasion shortly after he arrived in Haworth he was already at prayer when his servant rose at 5am. Then he went to a nearby house for 'religious exercises' with some of his parishioners, then home for more prayers, then to the church where he suddenly fell unconscious. When he recovered he was reported as being 'in a great rapture'. He proclaimed, 'I have had a glorious vision from the Third Heaven'. He spoke for five hours at the afternoon service and because his words were so earnest and heartfelt people flocked to hear him.

In a 'quiet' week Grimshaw would preach fourteen times; a busy week involved him in anything up to thirty meetings. He would speak anywhere, in any house he was invited to visit. When he preached in his own church people would come ten or more miles—whatever the weather or difficulty—to hear him. Often he would have 300 to 500 communicants at a service, but he would still, if necessary, tramp miles over the lonely moor just to visit an elderly or invalid person unable to come to the church. Given a pleasant summer's day the congregation swelled to several thousand. Obviously they could not all get into the church at one time, so the preachers would go outside to them or repeat the service over and over until all had heard.

Grimshaw was fearless: 'The Fear of the Lord,' he said, 'is far more powerful than the Fear of any man.' During the singing of the psalm before his sermon he would regularly clear the drinkers out of the public houses of Haworth and into the church, wielding a dog-whip if necessary. More than one 'miracle' is attributed to him. He had frequently protested at the annual three-day horse-racing event in Haworth which, admittedly, attracted the scum of the earth to the village. His protestations had no effect until he resorted to a mighty prayer to the Almighty that He would stop the races. A three-day-long deluge swamped Haworth. The event was never held again.

Grimshaw was in touch with Wesley from the start. He had been incumbent of Haworth for just ten days when John Wesley delivered his first sermon in Yorkshire—at Birstall Hill ('to several hundreds of plain people', he said) on 26 May 1742, and five years later Wesley arrived in Haworth for the first time. He returned regularly afterwards, and each time the congregation was larger.

Wesley was received rapturously in most places throughout his travels in the area. The first recorded meeting of Methodists in Todmorden (significantly on Todmorden Edge) came in 1748 and the next year Wesley carried the message on into Lancashire. The Wesleyans who established the Temple chapel at Summit, Littleborough, traced their formation to Wesley's visit of 1749; more properly the setting of their Society can be attributed to a visit from the redoubtable William Grimshaw in 1747. In *The Life of William Grimshaw* there is a reference which insists, 'Mr Grimshaw had introduced the preaching into a dark and ignorant part of Lancashire called Deanhead.' The 'Deanhead' of 1747 is the Summit of today and even now, in this borderland between Lancashire and Yorkshire, the Summit chapel comes within the Todmorden Methodist circuit whereas the chapels lower down in Littleborough come within the jurisdiction of Rochdale.

Wesley may have been welcomed in the 'dark and ignorant' upland village of Summit, but he was definitely most unwelcome in the more sophisticated Rochdale. In his journals he reports:

I rode, at the request of John Bennett, to Rochdale in Lancashire. As soon as ever we entered the town, we found the streets lined on both sides with multitudes of people, shouting, cursing, blaspheming and gnashing with their teeth. Perceiving it would not be practical to preach abroad, I went into a large room open to the street and called aloud 'Let the wicked forsake his way and the unrighteous man his thoughts.' The Word of God prevailed over the fierceness of Man. None opposed or interrupted; and there was a very remarkable change in the behaviour of the people as we afterwards went through the town.

Other Nonconformist sects arose and grew in stature; the Baptists were well established in the area by the middle of the eighteenth century. The Reverend James Hartley preached his particular brand of religion as strongly as Grimshaw at West Lane Chapel, and at Wainsgate Chapel Dr Fawcett thundered long. The first pastor of the chapel at Wainsgate, built in 1750, was one Richard Smith, who openly acknowledged the inspiration he had gained from William Grimshaw.

It was Grimshaw himself who built the first Wesleyan Chapel in Haworth, opened in 1758. A stone in the rebuilt chapel attests to this fact and another quotes one of his thunderous pronouncements: 'To us, to live is Christ. To die is gain.'

Resounding catechisms like this have driven themselves hard into the soul of succeeding generations of Northerners, but at the same time there are echoes of the distinctive Northern humour about some of William Grimshaw's pronouncements. It is reported that he once arrived as a visiting preacher and was courteously welcomed by the churchwarden. During the ensuing conversation the churchwarden casually mentioned that the local congregation was not over-fond of long sermons and hinted that Mr Wesley never preached more than an hour. Grimshaw saw the point immediately, but replied, 'Mr Wesley, God bless him, can do as much in one hour as I can do in two!'

In the early spring of 1763 there was an outbreak of plague in Haworth and there were many deaths. Grimshaw went about the village visiting the sick and ministering to the dying until, in April, he himself caught the fever and died. He was buried not at Haworth, but at the chapel at Luddenden, a few miles away over the moors.

Haworth went on to become a major manufacturing centre for

the woollen trade, at one time second only to Bradford (and ahead of Leeds and Halifax) in the amount of wool used there for worsteds. Its vicars continued to be cast in the radical mould and it was to this busy little town, still reverberating, one feels, to the thunder of Mr Grimshaw's admonitions, that, in 1821, the Reverend Patrick Brontë brought his sick wife and six small children.

Heptonstall Chapel

Grimshaw died in 1763, and the following summer Wesley paid one of his periodic visits, this time preaching within the shell of the half-finished chapel at Heptonstall, just over the hill from Haworth. This was to be one of the new-pattern 'steeple houses'—Wesley had decreed that his chapels should be octagon-shaped if the site allowed and such chapels had already been built at Norwich in 1757, at Rotherham in 1761 and at Whitby the following year.

These houses were not designed to be alternatives to the regular churches but additions to them. The principle was that the people would attend the church first, then move to the preaching house for further Methodist teaching.

The roof for the Heptonstall Octagon was made at Rotherham by the man who had designed the roof for the chapel there and was brought to Heptonstall by a column of pack-horses (surely a pioneer example of pre-fabrication), but by 1802 it was already inadequate for the swelling congregations and it was extended by lengthening the centre walls, unfortunately destroying the original octagon shape.

This building, first consecrated on 5 July 1764, still stands close by the hilltop church at Heptonstall. It pre-dates the City Temple in London by some fifteen years and is said to be the oldest Methodist place of worship still in regular use.

5
'GOD SAVE KING GEORGE AND BLESS OUR TRADE'

Wesley, Grimshaw and the rest preached to and travelled about a perceptibly changing world. Mills powered by the fast moving Pennine streams were beginning to appear; one of the earliest, Hudson Mill in the Colden valley on the north side of Calderdale, had been built as a corn mill in 1738 when William Grimshaw was still in the curacy of Todmorden. During the second half of the century mills were to proliferate throughout the area.

On his first visit to Calderdale and the Roch valley in 1747 Wesley would have had to use the old pack-horse tracks across the moors and endure the perils of the Reddyshore Scoutgate to reach Littleborough from Todmorden. By 1750 the road from Todmorden along Calderdale to Halifax was turnpiked, but it was not until 1760 that the roads along the valleys from Todmorden towards Burnley and Rochdale were built.

The old pack-horse tracks were desperately inadequate and the costs of carrying goods away from the expanding industrial centres within the Pennines were prohibitive. From prehistoric times, rivers had provided a reliable means of transport—in many cases the only reliable means—and Yorkshire was fortunate in having the Ouse, the Aire and the Calder. York had grown up at the head of navigation on the Ouse and recent excavations there have shown that in Viking times it was a considerable trading and shipping centre. The Trent gave access from the lower Ouse to the Midlands and the Romans had cut the Fossdyke canal to link the Trent to Lincoln.

Lancashire was less fortunate. Its rivers were mostly short and swift-flowing, tumbling down from the steep western scarp of the Pennines and offering little scope for navigation.

Surveys were carried out as early as 1712 to consider navigational improvements to the Mersey and Irwell and the River Douglas (to give access to the Ribble estuary for the coal-field around Wigan) and the works were in hand by 1720.

The Pennine area was, however, still remote and people were beginning to realise the desperate need for better links with the outside world. In 1734 a petition to Parliament called attention to the deplorable state of the road over Blackstonedge. It stated:

> ... by reason of the nature of the soil and the narrowness of the road in several places and of the many heavy carriages frequently passing it has become so exceeding deep and ruinous that in the winter season and often in summer, many parts thereof are impassable for wagons, carts and other wheeled carriages and very dangerous to travellers.

The alternative route through the pass to Todmorden and along Calderdale was no less hazardous. The old pack-horse track ran from a junction in the centre of Littleborough across the fields to Town House, then climbed up on to the valley 'shelf' at Calderbrook. From here it climbed again to the rim of the Summit Pass and then dropped precipitously to the valley floor again at Walsden. The Roch valley above Littleborough was undrained, making it virtually marshland and notoriously vulnerable to sudden and catastrophic flash-flooding. There was no road directly along the valley until 1824—twenty-five years after the building of the Rochdale Canal had drained the marsh (and only a year before the opening of the Railway Age!).

The Navigations

By the mid-1750s, the merchants of Halifax were pressing for improvements to the lower Calder to enable them to ship goods out by way of the Aire and Calder Navigation; in 1757, and after a great deal of wrangling about water rights, Parliamentary approval was obtained for the construction of the Calder and Hebble Navigation, from a junction with the Aire and Calder at Wakefield up to Sowerby Bridge at the foot of the hill on which Halifax stands.

John Smeaton, fresh from his triumph as the builder of the third Eddystone lighthouse, was engaged to survey the line of the navigation and prepare plans. Work began shortly afterwards, but flooding was a constant problem and much of the early work was subsequently washed away. The navigation was not fully complete until 1770.

Meanwhile, spasmodic improvements were being made to the

trans-Pennine roads. The Blackstonedge road had been turn-piked immediately after the petition to Parliament and some improvements had been made to the road between Todmorden and Littleborough. The 'improvement' often consisted of laying a second line of paving stones parallel to the original pack-horse paving, at a distance of roughly the length of a cart-axle from the first line. The notoriously difficult Reddyshore Scoutgate was 'improved' in this way, the wheels of the carts ending up a hair's-breadth away from a sheer drop; in some places the paving slabs disappeared altogether and the carts made their way across smooth (and sometimes wet and icy) bed-rock!

Gradually, sections were rebuilt, gradients eased and some diversions made. At Calderbrook, for instance, a cut-off was made to by-pass the hamlet of Higher Calderbrook. Part of the redundant section of road remains and is said to be the best-preserved stretch of improved pack-horse paving in the country. A new section of road was eventually built, dropping to the valley floor at Steanorbottom and running on to Walsden, and the Reddyshore Scoutgate eliminated. Finally, the Calderbrook turnpike was established in 1783. This road diverged from the Rochdale–Halifax turnpike just west of Littleborough and ran direct to Calderbrook along the hillside above the village. The old track from Littleborough joined it at the top of the appropri-ately named 'Newgate' Brow.

Clearly, though, the real answer to the transport problem was the use of canals and these were appearing on either side of the Pennines. In 1737 a group of Manchester businessmen, some of whom were connected with the Mersey and Irwell Navigation, proposed the improvement of the Worsley Brook and then in 1755 an Act of Parliament was obtained to improve the Sankey Brook linking St Helens to the River Mersey. The Worsley project did not materialise at that time but the Sankey Brook plan went ahead. It was adapted to provide for a separate channel alongside the brook itself. This channel, it is generally accepted, was the first 'true' canal (as opposed to improved river naviga-tion). It was opened throughout most of its length in 1757—the same year in which the Calder and Hebble received its Parlia-mentary sanction.

By the time the Sankey Brook Canal opened completely, work

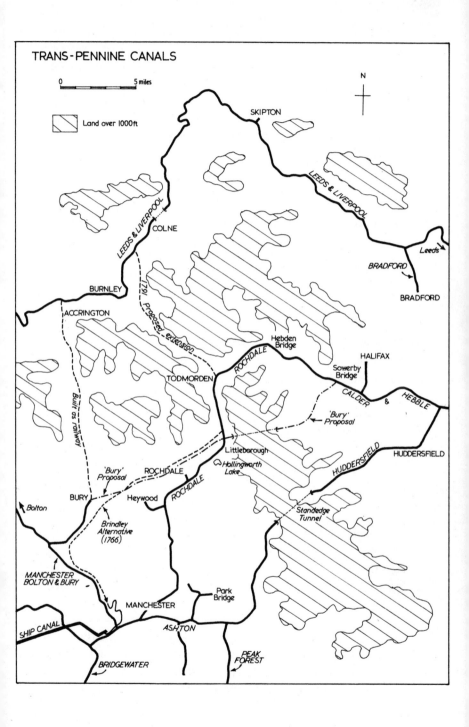

was in progress on a canal between Worsley and Manchester. Francis Egerton, Duke of Bridgewater, owned coal mines at Worsley and saw the desirability of carrying his product to Manchester by water. The first proposal, in 1759, was for a canal entirely on the north side of the Irwell to Salford, but a change in plan carried it over the river by means of an aqueduct to terminate at Castlefield, near the site of the Roman Mancunium fort on the southern edge of the city.

Brindley

Brindley, the engineer of the Bridgewater Canal, was an original genius. An illiterate millwright, he was to be the inspiration behind the construction of the English canals network. It is said that his illiteracy was his salvation. Since he could not read he could not be influenced by the designs or theories of others; therefore his concepts had to be original. The Bridgewater Canal opened in 1761 and was an immediate and phenomenal success. The price of coal in Manchester dropped dramatically; the boats could carry large quantities cheaply, and, considering the appalling state of the roads, rapidly.

In 1766 two important meetings were held within six weeks of each other. In July a meeting was arranged at the Sun Inn, Bradford 'to consider the proper means and ways to effect a navigation that will connect the East and West Seas'. This was to become the Leeds and Liverpool Canal. Then, on 10 August, a meeting was called at the Union Flag Inn in Rochdale to consider 'making surveys plans and estimates of the intended canal from the Calder and Hebble Navigation at Sowerby Bridge to the Bridgewater Canal at Manchester'. Again, reference was made to connecting the East and West Seas.

The Leeds and Liverpool committee appointed John Longbotham, a pupil of Smeaton (who was, at the time, completing the work on the Calder and Hebble), to carry out a first survey. The Rochdale meeting agreed to approach James Brindley— still, at this time, in the employment of the Duke of Bridgewater.

Of the two, the Leeds and Liverpool project was by far the more ambitious. It was to run north-westwards, up Airedale, then across the high land between Skipton and Colne, skirt the

Rossendale Fells and then make its way across the Lancashire Plain to Liverpool. The canal, as finally constructed, was 127 miles long. By contrast, the Rochdale scheme seemed comparatively straightforward, even allowing for the rugged Pennine terrain through which it would run. It would, after all, be only a quarter the length of the Leeds and Liverpool and would be linking with two existing waterways.

The Rochdale Proposal

The instigator of the meeting at the Union Flag Inn in Rochdale was one Richard Townley of Belfield, Rochdale, and at the meeting he and forty-seven other local prominent citizens—including the then Lord of the Manor, Lord Byron, and Colonel Beswick-Royds of Pike House, Littleborough—subscribed a sum of £237.4s.6d to enable the survey to get under way.

The canal proposals aroused immediate interest and the manufacturers of Bury urged the Rochdale men to build the canal via their town. For them a canal running parallel to the River Roch down to Bury, then down the Irwell valley to Manchester was logical. This would have made the distance from Rochdale to Manchester over twenty miles—twice as far as by the direct route—and Townley recognised that this would tend to discriminate against the districts between Rochdale and Sowerby Bridge. He declined to accept the case put forward by the men of Bury, but instructed Brindley (one feels with little enthusiasm!) to prepare a survey for a canal via Bury as well as one on a direct line.

Brindley submitted his estimates for the two routes in October 1766. Both used the Calderdale–Summit route as far as Littleborough and then one continued direct to Manchester by running along the eastern side of the Roch valley to Rochdale, then south to Middleton and finally down a part of the Irk valley to Manchester (slightly to the west of the line of the canal as built). The other proposed route ran along the other side of the valley, skirting Rochdale to the north, past Bamford Hall to descend to the valley at Gristlehurst. It then ran south of Bury and down the Irwell valley to Manchester. In both cases he submitted estimates for both broad and narrow canals.

Brindley's survey and estimates for the canal by the 'short' route from Reddy-shore (Summit) by way of Langley to Manchester. The canal as built is much on this line from Summit to Middleton, then runs to the east of the line proposed by Brindley.

James Brindley's Estimate of ye Intended Navigation from Sowerby Bridge to Manchester, taken in October 1766

Land 31 miles 555 yds allowing 8 Statute Acres to 1 mile is 250, 48 Acres at 40£ p Acre	10019	4	0
Digging to Chelburn 24640 yds at 4s p yd	4928	0	0
Digging from Chelburn to Manchester by Langley 3047 yds @ 3s p yd	4570	10	0
Bridges, Tunnels Gates etc ye whole length at 210£ per mile	6575	2	0
78 Locks/each 12 feet/at 500£ p lock	39000	0	0

Extra Work

Bridges and tunnel at Sowerby Bridge Dixon's Scar	500	0	0
Hollingholm Wood & Brook 400£	800	0	0
Luddendenfoot or Boy's Scar 450£ Anchor Brook 70£	520	0	0
Mythamroyd & Bridge 450£ Errenden Brook 150£	600	0	0
Palace House Car or Wood 250£ Hepton Bridge 500£	750	0	0
Mytham Bridge 100£ Rattenstall Bank 600£	700	0	0
Hebble Bridge 100£ a narrow passage 60£	160	0	0
Mr Thomas Gibson's Mill 160£ Gawksholm Brook etc 400£	560	0	0
New Bridge at Ramsden Clough 300£ Reddishore 150£	450	0	0
Heallee's Brook 200£ at brown 10£	210	0	0
Beal Brook 1834£ 10s Do at Bridge 250£	2084	0	0
Wallhead Brook & Bridge 680£ 14s 6d	680	14	6
Mr Taylor's Mill 86£ 2s Do a Bridge 20£	106	2	0
Lower Hey 5£ Castleton Moor 350£	355	0	0
Crowledges 45£ Hatty Green 20£ Stakhill 5£	070	0	0
Coney Green 77£ 16s Nr school Rooden Lane 360£	437	16	0
Back of Salford 800£ 2 Bridges over ye river 400£	4800	0	0

The total estimate For a Narrow Canal	79146	18	6
Do For a Broad Canal	105529	4	48

By Langley

Brindley's estimate for a canal via Bury. Besides being longer than the direct route, this line along the Roch valley had some substantial engineering problems. Note the figures for works at Heybrook, Bamford, the tunnel at Ringley and the bridges across the Irwell.

James Brindley's Estimate of ye intended navigation from Sowerby Bridge to Manchester, taken in October 1766

By Bury—Northern Most Course

Land 35 miles = 205 yds allowing 8 Statute			
Acres to a mile, is 281.64 Acres at 40£ p	11265	12	0
Digging 24640 yds to Chelburn at 4s p yd	4928	0	0
Digging 37320 yds to Manchester at 3s p yd	5598	2	0
For Bridges, Tunnels, Gates etc			
35 mls; 205 yd at 210£ p mile	7393	1	0
78 locks/each 12 foot/at 500£ a lock	39000	0	0
	68184	15	0

Extra Work

Bridges and Tunnel at Sowerby Bridge	500	0	0
Dixon's Scar 400£ Hollinholm Wood & Brook 400£	800	0	0
Luddonden Foot or Boys Scar 450£	450	0	0
Anchor Brook 70£ Mythamroyd Bridge 450£	520	0	0
Palace House Car 250£ Errenden Brook 150£	400	0	0
Hebden Bridge 500£ Mytham Bridge 100	600	0	0
Rattenstall Bank 600£ Hebble Bridge 100	700	0	0
A narrow passage 60£ Mr Gibson's Mill 170	230	0	0
Digging a Hill 100£ Mr Gibson's Mill 160	260	0	0
Gawksholm Mill and Brook	400	0	0
New Bridge at Ramsden Clough	300	0	0
Reddishore 150£ Heybrook 3848; 19s	3998	19	0
Entering Cronkyshaw	4445	0	0
Spotland Brook 2521£; 18 do a Bridge 300£	2821	18	0
Digging beyond Dixon's Fould	113	9	0
1st Clough at Bamford Hall and Bridge	6609	0	0
Digging a Hill	647	17	0
2nd Clough and Bridge Near Bamford	1290	8	0
Entering Gristlehurst	200	0	0
Bridge over Irwell below Bury	1500	0	0
A Tunnel 1666 yds at 4 guineas a yard	6997	0	0
Two bridges near Wringley	2000	0	0
The Broken Bank Near Salford	262	10	0
A Bridge to ye Quay	2000	0	0
Total for a narrow canal	102230	15	0
Total for a broad canal	136307	13	4

The business men of Bury kept up the pressure on Townley, soliciting the help of the Derby family, the traditional overlords of Lancashire. Lord Strange tried to persuade Townley to adopt the Bury line, but Townley and his Rochdale friends clearly preferred the more direct route. In any case, the difference in cost was considerable; a narrow canal by the shorter route would cost under £80,000 compared with over £100,000 by the Bury route and for a broad canal £105,000 compared with £136,000. Brindley had indicated that the Bury proposal would require a 1,666 yard long tunnel near Ringley (at four guineas per yard) and £7,000 would be swallowed up by this one feature alone.

The opposition to Townley's short route was implacable. Backed by the Derbys and the powerful interests they represented, the men of Bury even threatened to build their own canal. Townley was baulked at every turn; under extreme pressure and aware of the problems caused by the disastrous flooding of the Calder and Hebble he was persuaded to suspend his plans for a canal to link Manchester direct to Sowerby Bridge. It was to be twenty-five years before the plans were revived.

Meanwhile, work began to the north. In 1770 Parliament sanctioned the construction of the Leeds and Liverpool Canal. Under this Act the canal would have run from Foulridge to Padiham, then down the valleys of the Lancashire Calder and the Ribble to Walton-le-Dale, Leyland, Mawdesley, Parbold and Newburgh to Liverpool—a much wider sweep west and south and away from the towns of Accrington and Blackburn. It looked very much as though the circuitous Leeds and Liverpool Canal would be the first to link Lancashire and Yorkshire. In the event there were many delays, and changes of route affected the progress of the works and it was not until 1819 that the Leeds and Liverpool Canal was fully open to traffic. The most noticeable change in the canal's course was that it was re-aligned to run through the growing industrial centres of Accrington and Blackburn, which is surely an indication of the importance these towns had assumed after the first canal proposals of 1770.

The Growth of Industry

By 1790 the effect of industrialisation was being felt throughout the South Pennines. Factories were beginning to appear and around 1785 cotton began to arrive from America. 'Lancashire' came to mean cotton and 'Yorkshire' wool, but here in the borderland both industries have always operated side by side. Todmorden, for instance, was particularly strong on cotton and Littleborough was peculiarly reliant on wool. Not until one got down to Rochdale or Halifax did the traditional 'division' become apparent.

Thanks to the Spinning Jenny, the Water Frame and so on, spinning was already becoming mechanised and the spinners, but not weavers, were drawn into the new factories. The first factory in Todmorden was John Fielden's Clough Mill, built in 1786. Soon afterwards, Joshua Fielden (significantly one of the Quaker Fieldens) leased, or perhaps built, a small manufactory at Laneside, consisting of three or four three-storey dwellings. In 1790 a man with the familiar 'borderland' name of Crossley built a small mill at Knowl and a number of other structures appeared. But Crossley's mill was different; it was probably the first mill to be built down in the valley in what was becoming the town of Todmorden.

All the same, most people still lived in small hamlets on the valley shelf, Shore, Bottomley, Lumbutts and Mankinholes, and water was the main source of power for the mills (although Joshua Fielden's Laneside had already been equipped with a steam-engine).

Spinning was mechanised long before weaving, which meant that much of the traditional 'system' survived. The spun yarn was put out to individual hand-loom weavers and then the finished pieces were collected; merchants would often have a number of weavers (often spread over a large area) subcontracted to them. The 'finishing' of the cloth (bleaching and fulling and so on) was also mechanised early on; but the proud and fiercely independent hand-loom weaver dominated the industry until well into the next century.

Halifax Piece Hall

The finished cloth would be taken to the market, perhaps to Halifax where a splendid new Piece Hall was opened on 1

January 1779. This building was, and remains, one of the architectural gems of the North of England. A number of designs had been suggested, including a circular one, but the difficulties of building such a structure on sloping ground were readily appreciated by the people of Halifax and the plan finally accepted was that of a local architect, Thomas Bradley. Strangely enough, Bradley was Surveyor to the Calder and Hebble Navigation.

Bradley's plan was for a rectangular structure roughly 110yd by 90yd, with an open courtyard in the centre and over 300 small rooms opening off the galleries around it. The style of architecture adopted was a distinctive 'Roman-Renaissance Adapted'. Those who had subscribed towards the cost of building the Piece Hall were given the first option of leasing a room at an annual rent of around £28. The smaller merchant, or perhaps the individual weaver, paid a levy for the right to exhibit his goods on the grassed-over central courtyard.

Inevitably, a committee, made up from the occupiers, was set up to administer the Hall and the rules it devised were extremely strict. The Hall was open for business only between 10am and 12 noon every Saturday. From 8am until 9.45am and between 12.30pm and 4pm, either a cart with one horse only, or packhorses, were allowed into the courtyard to deliver and take away goods. Promptly at 11.55am a bell was rung, and this continued until noon. At the end of that time anyone caught still selling or buying cloth was fined the sum of 5/-. Anyone with a horse or cart inside the Hall during the two hours devoted to business was, again, fined 5/-. Anyone breaking a pane of glass was fined 3d and there was a fine for sweeping rubbish out of the rooms through the railings (that is, on to the heads of the people in the courtyard below).

In 1971 an opportunity arose to restore the Piece Hall. Government grants were made available for the cleaning and restoration of buildings and Halifax tied the refurbishing of the Piece Hall to a scheme to develop a new wholesale market. The Piece Hall now houses an industrial museum, an art gallery and restaurants. Most importantly, it keeps its commercial purpose and many of the small sale-rooms have become craft workshops and antique shops.

Halifax Piece Hall represents a quite specific way of life.

Because of the particular system of manufacture involved, both buyer and seller had to travel—often many miles—to be at Halifax on time for the market. They needed accommodation, and both sides of the trade selected particular inns where they could be approached outside the rigid business hours imposed by the Piece Hall administrators. Business stationery would give the inn used by the businessman as well as the room at the Piece Hall occupied by him. The inns that grew up around the Piece Hall—and there were over twenty of them—were quite different from inns in other parts of the country. As much, if not more, business would be done in the inns of Halifax as was done in the Piece Hall.

When the Piece Hall opened, the merchants gathered for what was undoubtedly a great occasion. Buildings on the approaches had been repainted and hung with garlands of thorn, mistletoe and holly. The courtyard was crowded with people and the whole splendid ceremony was celebrated in song. The composition shows a very correct order of priorities:

> God Save King George *and bless our Trade*,
> Let not our prayers be vain,
> May all our Foes to Friends be turn'd
> And Peace *and Plenty* reign.

6
WARP, WEFT AND WATER

In view of the changed circumstances brought about by the expansion of industry, a group of businessmen met in Hebden Bridge in 1790 to discuss the possibility of extending the Calder and Hebble Navigation as far as Hebden Bridge. A group of businessmen from Rochdale attended the meeting and the whole question of a canal through the Pennines was revived.

On 10 June 1791 a meeting was held at the Roebuck Inn, Rochdale, and it was resolved that an application to Parliament should be made as soon as possible. Richard Townley's plan still existed, but Brindley was dead and it was resolved to engage John Rennie as surveyor and engineer of the proposed canal and to invite William Crossley of Brighouse to assist him. On 19 August Rennie was directed additionally to:

> ... survey a branch from this intended canal, from or near Todmorden to the Limeworks in the neighbourhood of Colne in such direction as he shall think most eligible; and another branch to some convenient place near the Parish Church of Rochdale. And that he continue his survey from the place where he has now left off by the south line described in the plan of Mr Brindley to some convenient point, near the Town of Manchester, from whence a connection may be made either to the canal of His Grace the Duke of Bridgewater, or the Navigation of the River Irwell, as at some future meeting of the committee shall be decided upon; And that he also survey a Branch from some convenient point of the said canal to connect as nearly as possible with the Town of Oldham.

This directive seems to indicate that the canal's Rochdale proposers had some ambitious plans in mind. The branch from Todmorden would link their canal with the Leeds and Liverpool; the proposed branch to Oldham, one suspects, was designed to get the merchants of that town behind the Rochdale project and thwart the anticipated opposition from the men of Bury. That opposition was not long in coming. A few months previously, the Manchester, Bolton and Bury Canal Act sanctioned the construction of a canal between those three towns; the men of Bury now proposed extending their canal up the Roch valley to join the line of the proposed 'Rochdale' canal through the Pennines.

On receiving Rennie's findings, the committees from Hebden Bridge and Rochdale combined and began to raise capital to launch the project to provide (as their proposals elegantly stated):

> ... the means of opening of a certain communication for the conveyance of goods, ware and merchandise, coal, stone and slate between the East and West seas whereby the trade and manufactures of many very considerable Towns and Places will be very greatly promoted and facilitated and the agriculture of a very populous country materially assisted by being supplied with lime and other manure at a moderate expense.

The committee, although presenting a combined case, kept its two separate sections. One met in Rochdale and the other, responsible for the (Calder and) Hebble end, met at a hostelry near Hebden Bridge, which still exists, now called the Stubbing Wharf Inn. The area is now known as Hebble End.

With the publication of the proposals to connect Sowerby Bridge and Manchester by canal and the immediate counter-proposals by the supporters of the 'Bury' plans began a protracted and complex series of rival projects, negotiations, accusations and compromises which were to last three years and to result in two failed Parliamentary Bills before the final Act that sanctioned the construction of the canal.

The Mill-owners

Not unnaturally, the owners of the many water-powered mills along the line of the canal were disturbed by the proposals. The promoters intended to divert streams feeding the rivers to supply their canal and rely only to a limited extent on catchment reservoirs of their own. The mill-owners (particularly those in the Calder valley) insisted that they needed all the available water supplies to power their mills and facilitate their finishing processes. They put forward a powerful argument:

... there are at present on the said rivers upwards of thirty mills within the distance of forty miles for the milling of woollen cloths, scribbling and spinning of wool and cotton and the grinding of corn which produce to the Proprietors upwards of £10,000 per annum, and these mills in time of drought experience considerable loss for want of water. Many of these are not able to work more than twelve or fourteen hours a day, and should a diminution of water, sufficient to supply a canal take place, the petitioners apprehend may nearly be rendered useless in the summer months and the Manufacturers be obliged (as has been the case within four or five years) to carry their cloths to distant mills, on other rivers to be milled; and that the trade and manufacturers of that part of the country have of late greatly increased, and, there is reason to hope are in a state of progressive increase, that the rivers Calder and Hepton in their present state are not equal to the powers wanted by the several mills situate thereon and if a diminution of water in these rivers takes place, these mills must inevitably be very materially injured, as well as the trade and manufactures of the neighbourhood.

This convoluted argument paints a graphic picture of the critical state of affairs existing at the time. Water was used over and over again, from the mills high on the moors—often 1,000ft up—to the newer mills rising on the rivers themselves. On the Cheesden Brook near Rochdale, for instance, there were fourteen mills, using the water for power, bleaching, dyeing, fulling and printing.

The promoters of the rival canal from Bury now introduced a new proposal. They suggested a canal up the Roch valley to a point just north of Littleborough where it would turn east and tunnel under Blackstonedge to emerge in the Ryburn valley and makes its way to Sowerby Bridge via Ripponden. On the face of it, this was an attractive proposal, particularly for the mill-owners on the overworked Calder; none of their water would be taken for the canal and they would still have access if a short branch canal were built sufficiently far up the valley from Sowerby Bridge.

The Blackstonedge Alternative

The promoters of the 'Blackstonedge' line also had powerful support and were represented by Peel and Stanley when the first Rochdale Canal Bill came before Parliament. Their arguments,

plus the petitioning of the mill-owners (which the Rochdale promoters had totally underestimated), resulted in the Bill being
defeated on its Second Reading by sixty votes to twenty-two.

The multiplicity of proposals regarding the canal through the
Pennines has confused and tantalised enthusiasts as well as historians right up to the present day. Did the supporters of the
'Blackstonedge' proposal really believe such a tunnel was a practical proposition, or was it simply a move to undermine the
'Rochdale' plans? Certainly detailed plans were drawn, one
showing a junction between the two canals (one direct, the other
from Manchester via Bury) at Sladen, the point at which the
canal would turn east. At that point there is an old quarry known
as 'th' Backin' Hole' and a basin is shown here, in which boats
would wait to make the passage through the tunnel. The junction would have been at the foot of Lydgate Clough, one of the
side valleys biting into the main ridge; a little way up the clough
stood a pub, officially called The Woodcock, but known locally
as 'Th' Gap' or, more significantly, 'Th' Water Yate' (Gate).
Admittedly, the feeder channel for the present canal runs hard
alongside the site of the pub, but 'gate' means 'road'. Was the
pub's nickname an echo of the proposal to build a canal up the
clough? Perhaps the surveyors for the line frequented it?

Townhouse Warehouse

Brindley's original proposals for a canal via Bury and the similar
line of later proposals would have taken the canal along the
western side of the valley of the Roch—Heybrook and Cronkeyshaw are both mentioned on the first schedules. Both these
places are relatively high above Rochdale, so Brindley intended
the canal to be at something like 500ft as it passed Littleborough.
On this contour stands a building which raises what is at least a
tantalising—though totally unofficial—possibility.

A group of buildings known as Old or Lower Townhouse
stands at the foot of Gorsey Hill, a short distance from the centre
of Littleborough and at the point where the old pack-horse track
began its climb up on to the valley 'shelf' and Calderbrook. The
structure consists of an old farmhouse, barns and shippons and a
substantial building characteristic of the three-storey weavers'

cottages seen all over the area. Alongside the cottages is a building known as the Warehouse. It has been long assumed that the building was used as a Takkin' In Shop, or simply as a warehouse to be used in connection with the farm. But it is an impressive structure, three storeys high with arched doorways on each floor and has more the characteristics of a canal warehouse—one wonders if this was a piece of speculative building by the owners of Townhouse, in the hope that the canal would come their way. The Calderbrook turnpike was not built until 1783 and until then the main 'road' from Littleborough would have crossed the canal at that point—an ideal situation for a town wharf; even after the building of the turnpike a wharf here would have been a mere couple of hundred yards off the main highway and easily accessible from the town across the fields.

The Second Application

However, before the canal was to be built there were two further Parliamentary debates to be endured, as well as an untold amount of argument and negotiation. Undeterred by the rejection of the first Bill (although probably chastened by the experience), the Rochdale promoters held another meeting in August 1792 and resolved to try again. They approached the Duke of Bridgewater in an attempt to enlist his support (which he had refused at an earlier date). He agreed to their suggestion of a link with his canal, but proposed an enormous toll—3s 8d on every ton of cargo passing his basins.

The second proposals laid before Parliament included some safeguards for the beleaguered mill-owners of the Calder valley. It was suggested that only *excess* water should be fed into the canal from the side-streams; under normal conditions water would be conducted straight under the canal along its normal course. This was a considerable concession, but was rejected as 'a specious offer' and totally unacceptable by the mill-owners.

However, the opposition from the mill-owners was not as implacable as it had been. One group—substantially those in the Todmorden area—actually supported the proposals. They were, after all, most in need of the cheap and reliable transport offered by a canal and least at risk, being near the headwaters of the rivers. The main body of mill-owners in the Calder valley was still opposed to the proposals, and lobbied again in the same terms as before. But a third group entered the battle and Parliament was faced with fragmented opposition to two rival proposals. The 'Bury' men reintroduced their plan for a tunnel under Blackstonedge and a canal down the Ryburn valley and further hinted that they had reached an agreement with the disgruntled mill-owners along the line. Parliament (possibly totally confused by the whole complicated issue!) rejected both Bills, but this time the Rochdale proposal was defeated by a single vote.

The Rochdale men reappraised the plans. They enlisted support from a wide area—Liverpool, Wakefield, Leeds, Hull, even Coventry, Bristol and Gloucester. Specifically, they worked on an agreement with the owners of the water-powered mills. They agreed to draw the bulk of their supplies from the moors, from:

> so many reservoirs for the purpose of supplying the said canal and cuts respectively with water, in or upon the moors or commons called Blackstonedge, or any enclosed lands within a distance of three hundred yards from the said moors or commons as the Company of Proprietors shall think proper.

This extraordinary proposal, which was quite unprecedented, gave the Rochdale Canal Company a large and indefinite power over a vast area on the Pennine watershed. On it, they were eventually to build a gigantic network of reservoirs, which was far larger and more complex than any other canal constructed. In return for these rights the company was obliged to 'discharge from the said canal and Reservoirs for and towards the supply of the said mills, a quantity of water equal to double the quantity of water which shall be intercepted and diverted'.

With the benefit of hindsight, there seems to have been a deal of desperation in an agreement of this sort. Under the proposed Act the canal would be discharging from its reservoirs twice the quantity of water it would use. And in spite of the apparent restrictions on their use of water, the canal's promoters were getting their supplies on highly advantageous terms. The catchment areas were there and there was no competition at that time. The Rochdale Canal Company ultimately controlled an area of over 2,000 acres within the watershed of the River Calder and that alone yielded an average supply of 4 million gallons a day; in practice the compensatory water released into the Calder amounted to only 0.26 million gallons a day.

An extremely complex battle was coming to an end. It was nearly thirty years since the first meeting at the Union Flag Inn in Rochdale. Brindley had died and even Rennie was now engaged on other projects and had handed over to William Jessup. Other canals had fingered their way across England (although the Leeds and Liverpool Canal was not yet completed and a canal between Manchester and Huddersfield was still at proposal stage) and the turnpikes had largely replaced the old pack-horse tracks. In the intervening years the American colonies had become the United States and were shipping cotton to Lancashire in quantity. The first rotary-action steam engines were appearing in the new factories, suggesting the eventual replacement of the troublesome water-powered mills. Counterfeiting, which had been a major occupation in the Calder valley, had flourished and been suppressed. France was deep in revolution and the Piece Hall at Halifax alive with merchants and weavers.

Mitchell of Sowerby

Coincidentally, three weeks after the Rochdale Canal received Parliamentary sanction, a man called Thomas Mitchell, a worsted manufacturer of Higgin Chamber, Sowerby, drew up a list of his debtors and compiled an inventory of the contents of his house.

This notebook shows that earlier, in 1788, one of the Mitchells of Higgin Chamber was engaged in carting materials such as stone, lime and sand. Rather more surprising, it lists several loads of brick, which was a new material in the Pennines at the time. (The old Congregational Church in Halifax, built in 1772, is said to have been one of the first buildings built in this material.) The usual destination was Rochdale or 'Smae Bridge'—Smallbridge, between Littleborough and Rochdale and written the way it would be pronounced locally.

The Mitchell family lived at Higgin Chamber right through

the 'canal' period and saw the coming of the railway and the consequent development of the area. Thomas Mitchell had seven children, born between 1790 and 1801. The youngest, William, continued to live at Higgin Chamber. William's second child, Frances, was born in 1835, just about the time when a railway was again being talked about after earlier setbacks. His youngest child was born in 1845, after the railway had arrived and, indeed, after it had changed its name from the Manchester & Leeds to the Lancashire & Yorkshire.

Frances married Abraham Baldwin and went to live a short distance away at Rose Grove, Warley, just across the valley from Higgin Chamber and visible from it. The Mitchells had owned Higgin Mill, down in the valley below the village, but a note in the book tells us, 'Higgin Mill burned down September 5th 1856, beginning at about 20 minutes before 8 o'clock in the evening'.

Abraham and Frances Baldwin had five children. Their three sons were 'put to' the all-important engineering, an ancillary to the textile industry. Two sons moved away to Blackburn in Lancashire, where one worked for Yates & Thoms, world famous for their manufacture of mill-engines. The two daughters moved 'away' too, to Littleborough and only one child stayed in his native Yorkshire. In Littleborough, one daughter married a 'comer in' with the alien name of Parry. Of their children, their elder son, Fred, married a local girl with a name (Butterworth) that can be traced back 700 years on the western slopes of the Pennines. Their son chose the totally alien trade of writing!

The warp and weft of history weave a complicated pattern hereabouts, and when your name is Fielden, Cockroft, Mitchell, Baldwin (or even Parry) history is very close at hand!

7
'BY THE NEAREST PRACTICAL COURSE'

The Rochdale Canal Act was passed on 4 April 1794 and, the long battle over, work began at various points on the Yorkshire side immediately.

Parliament had made an important proviso. Instead of the 'narrow' canal (capable of taking the traditional 7ft wide boats) as originally envisaged, the Rochdale was to be built to 'broad' standards, big enough to take the 14ft wide barges in use on the Bridgewater Canal and the Calder and Hebble Navigation. This proviso, although wise, added many complications to the construction. Clearly, it was more expensive—Brindley had shown that in his original estimates of 1766—and the capital was less than adequate from the start. Supplying a broad canal with water was more difficult under any circumstances and in a hilly area considerably more problematical. The agreement regarding water rights reached with the Calder valley mill-owners made the whole question of water supply infinitely more difficult.

The original proposals (which remained substantially intact until the final Act) suggested five small reservoirs on the moors above the Summit Pass and two in the general Hollingworth area, plus, of course, water from the streams feeding the rivers. A map showing the plans for the Hollingworth reservoir indicates an additional reservoir in the Syke valley; in the event, Hollingworth was made much larger and the upper reservoir never built.

With the feeder-streams no longer available, the canal's engineers had to think in terms of a totally separate supply system and Parliament's insistence on a broad canal makes one wonder if it realised the terrain through which the canal was to run! A modern theory suggests that it did and that there were hopes that the whole project would fail through lack of capital; this would leave the way open to a takeover bid by the promoters of the Manchester, Bolton and Bury Canal's supporters. This canal had received Parliamentary approval in 1791, and although it was originally built as a 'narrow' canal, it was later converted to broad standards.

Progress on the canal's trans-Pennine section was impressive. By August 1798 it had reached Todmorden from Sowerby Bridge and by the end of the year it was substantially complete over the watershed and down as far as Rochdale. By any standards it was a substantial achievement; by the standards of the time it was phenomenal. There were few mechanical aids and even though the line of the canal had been surveyed over and over again the actual construction of this extremely difficult section posed some prodigious problems.

Immediately to the west of Sowerby Bridge the canal was cut into the rock face and raised above the river on a sizeable embankment. Here too (at Rose Grove) is one of the two tunnels. (Surprisingly, both Rochdale Canal tunnels are at the lower ends, rather than on the watershed as might be imagined.) At Hebden Bridge the canal crosses the Calder by means of an aqueduct which is insignificant by Pontcyssylte standards, but a substantial structure none the less. Rennie's design for the aqueduct is sophisticated and stylish; it relies for its effect entirely on its proportions and its clever use of stone of different colours.

West of Hebden Bridge the canal is constricted again and is cut into the rock on one side, the tow-path separating it from the steep drop to the river; it climbs on up the narrowing valley to Todmorden, then more steeply up the Walsden valley to the Summit Pass. Here it has been cut wider and deeper than necessary, making it a reservoir in itself, and it is here that the canal receives its supplies from the reservoirs on the moors above. In 1800, before the reservoir complex was complete, the water supply proved inadequate and the canal was closed from July to October; subsequently, the Blackstonedge reservoir embankment was raised.

The completion of the line down to Manchester from Rochdale was delayed by engineering difficulties and shortage of finance (applications to Parliament to raise additional capital were made in 1800 and 1806) and the canal was not fully open until 1804. Even so, it was the first trans-Pennine canal and fully justified its promoters' claims:

[The canal] would complete communications between the German Ocean and the Irish Channel by the nearest, practical course, bringing to the most populous districts in this Kingdom the hardwares of Sheffield, Birmingham and Wolverhampton, the potters wares of Burslem and Etruria, the glass of Stourbridge and Gainsborough, the hops, cider and fruit of the cider counties, the timber, wool and other materials for manufacture, the corn and other provisions of the most fertile parts of the counties of Lincoln, Oxford, Chester and York, and the various importations of the ports of Liverpool and Hull. Furthermore, it would supply these districts with the coals of Holmes Chapel, Walsden, Chadderton, Oldham and Worsley, with the stone of Ealand, Middle Hill and Oldham, and with the limestone of Knottingley, Buxton and North Wales and would carry from these districts large quantities of these minerals, together with nearly all the whole of their manufactures which are exported to all parts of the known world.

More prosaically, the canal was 33 miles long with its summit level 600ft above sea-level. It rose 315ft from Sowerby Bridge to this level, then fell over 500ft to Manchester, and although it was claimed to be the 'nearest, practical' course for trans-Pennine passage it was not the shortest, being eight miles longer than the route via Huddersfield, and it had the largest number of locks for its distance of any canal in the country. There were ninety-two locks between Sowerby Bridge and the junction with the Bridgewater Canal, each capable of taking craft 74ft × 14ft 2in × 4ft draft. There were upwards of 100 overbridges, 35 culverts, 2 tunnels, almost 1,500 linear yards of river retaining walls and 9 swing bridges.

By 1804, the Bridgewater Canal was open to Runcorn on the Mersey, so the 70ft barges could work through from Liverpool to Sowerby Bridge and the shorter Yorkshire boats could, in theory, work all the way through from Hull to the Mersey estuary. In order to save a proportion of the water needed to pass these shorter boats through the trans-Pennine section it was intended that the fifty locks east of Rochdale should be fitted with an additional 'inner' set of gates; the locks were constructed to allow for the fitting of these gates, but the evidence is that only Lock No 1 at Sowerby Bridge was actually so equipped, although many locks show evidence of a double set of lower-gate recesses.

The countryside is creeping back. Mill in Jumble Hole Clough on the boundary between Hebden Bridge and Todmorden

The Cloth Hall, Heptonstall. Built by the Waterhouse family of Shibden Hall, Halifax, in 1545–58. Hand-woven cloth pieces were brought here for sale until the Halifax Piece Hall was opened in 1779

Mankinholes and Stoodley Pike. Stoodley Pike was built to commemorate the Peace of Ghent in 1814. On the day the Crimean War broke out it collapsed – and again on 11 November 1918. Below are the twin villages of Mankinholes (in distance) and Lumbutts, typical hand-loom weaving hamlets on the pack-horse route along the southern edge of Calderdale. Withen Gate crossed the ridge close by the pike to drop to Cragg Vale. Silhouetted in the centre right is the Lumbutts Water Tower which had three water-powered wheels mounted vertically within it

Heptonstall Methodist Church. The oldest continuously used Methodist church in the world.

The Ceremonial Opening

The ceremonial opening of the completed canal, scheduled for 21 December 1804, turned out to be something less than a triumphant success. The directors hit upon the idea of opening the canal with a boat which had come from London to Rochdale entirely by inland waterway and an arrangement was made with Mr George Tindall, owner of the boat *Mayflower*. Unfortunately, the boat had first to make a passage from Hull to London with a cargo of Yorkshire coal; she was beaten back twice by storms off the Humber and only at the third attempt was she successful in reaching first the Medway and then Stanton Wharf in the Borough. As a result of the delays she was not in time to attend the opening ceremony.

All the same, the opening day was a great occasion. Boats left various points along the canal and assembled in Rochdale for the final procession down to Manchester. Men wore a blue and gold ribbon in their hats proclaiming 'Success to the Rochdale' and thousands of people lined the banks of the navigation to watch the boats go by. The weather had been cold and the frozen surface of the canal threatened to delay the proceedings. However, ice-breakers were provided and these led the procession from Rochdale.

At Failsworth, about four miles from the city centre, the band of the First Battalion, the Manchester and Salford Independent Volunteers, boarded the leading craft and enlivened the journey by playing popular tunes. Huge crowds greeted the boats—people lining the banks, crowding the bridges and even climbing on to the roofs of houses and mills—and the church bells rang, The *Mayflower* arrived quietly in Rochdale on 10 February 1805, unloaded part of its cargo and then went on to Manchester. Here the master reloaded with paving stones and on 14 February was in the Mersey having, at first, been refused admittance to the Duke of Bridgewater's Dock and that of the Mersey and Irwell. However, he arrived in Liverpool on the following tide where the *Mayflower* was visited by many people curious to see the first boat to arrive in the city by inland waterway all the way from London.

Water Supply

Water supply was again a problem after the opening of the Manchester section of the canal and it was not until 1827 that the canal had adequate supplies (in all but the driest seasons). In the intervening years a vast complex of reservoirs and feeder channels had been constructed in the Pennines above Littleborough. In all there were eight reservoirs; White Holme, Warland and Light Hazzles are grouped close together immediately to the north of the original Blackstonedge Reservoir and all are well over 1,200ft above sea-level. The Upper and Lower Chelburn Reservoirs were formed by damming off a side valley immediately to the south of the Summit level, whilst Hollingworth was made by building three embankments to enclose a natural hollow on the valley shelf south-east of Littleborough. From Hollingworth, water was pumped up into a feeder channel on the 600ft contour and along which it flowed four miles to the north along the valley side to discharge into the Summit level. Part of this feeder was underground; then for a short distance, Lydgate Brook provided a natural path for the water. The water was taken from the brook via a control-sluice into an artificial channel again. This curved round, high above the site of the abortive 'Tunnel Scheme' dock at Backing Hole and then ran more or less alongside the canal to the Summit Pool.

The final supply reservoir, Gaddings Dam, nearer Todmorden, is in fact two reservoirs. In 1824, in order to avoid the continuing 'annoyance and torment' suffered by the mill-owners in the Calder valley, the proprietors of the canal agreed to build Easterly Gaddings for the sole use of the mills, to be filled once a year from the feeders on Langfield Common and, subsequently, the mill-owners themselves built Westerly Gaddings alongside. This was to provide additional capacity and be a means of ensuring supply to the canal in dry periods. The supply from Gaddings was taken directly down Lumbutts Clough to the River Calder. In 1836, the canal's proprietors agreed that the discharge of the compensatory water should be confined to the sixty-nine (!) hours of the working week. Here again, the familiar name of Fielden occurs. The mill-owners' group was led by the Fielden Brothers of Waterside, Todmorden, who had a

major interest in the maintenance of water for power and processing in the valley. They used steam at their mill at Waterside
from an early date, but they also operated a further half-dozen
mills between Walsden and Mytholmroyd, halfway along the
Calder valley, and these relied on water power. This informal,
but powerful, pressure group of mill-owners was the earliest
local example of a combination determined to protect its
interests mutually. Although they could not entirely prevent the
canal from using certain feeder streams they ensured that water
taken from these streams was carefully controlled. Gauges were
fitted in each case and only when the gauge was 'filled' could
surplus water be taken into the canal. Twelve feeders only were
used (and only to this limited extent)—at Hawkeclough
(Mytholmroyd), Beamont, Paddock, Stoodley, Shaw, Lumbutts, Dobroyd, Dulesgate, Birks, Stonehouse, Warland and
Longlees Cloughs. Owler Clough Brook, coming in from the
Reddyshore side of the Summit level was, in fact, diverted into
the canal unchecked, but only the excess water from Lydgate
Brook, nearer Littleborough, was allowed into the canal; on the
other side an overflow sluice ensured that any surplus water in
the canal flowed back into the brook!

The water supply system to the Rochdale Canal remains a formidable achievement. In addition to the supply reservoirs,
something like twenty miles of feeder channel were built,
snaking across the moors leading to and linking the reservoirs.
The Broadhead Drain runs along the western side of Robin
Hood's Bed, taking water to the Blackstonedge Reservoir;
Castle Clough Drain takes water from Blackstonedge down to
the storage reservoirs at Chelburn. A major channel links Blackstonedge to the White Holme–Warland–Light Hazzles complex
which has its own channels bringing water from the moorland
catchment areas. The channels are massively constructed in gritstone masonry; even the tiny foot-bridges over them have a
certain architectural merit.

These engineering works for the canal gave a unique kind of
landscape to this part of the South Pennines. The maintenance
track alongside the feeder linking Blackstonedge to Light
Hazzles and Warland is now part of the Pennine Way, but is a
substantial road, one which is 1,200ft up with a view that

stretches out over the plain to the distant tower blocks of Manchester, almost twenty miles away. White Holme Reservoir, the largest of the complex on the high moor, feels utterly remote—a vast area of water on the very moor-top reflecting an enormous sky or merging into the mist and rain. The ground around has a primitive look to it; banks of deep-brown peat curving up to rough ling and heather, in places boulder-strewn, in others broken by a sudden outcropping of the gritstone. It prompted the lines:

> This is the last primeval land—
> Age-withered, wracked, resistant.
> Crying to cracked stone and
> Weeping iron streams, it dies—protestant.

But between the water and the land is often a slim beach of coarse near-white sand; it is perfectly possible to sun-bathe by the blue water 1,300ft above sea-level.

The Weyvers' Sayport

Hollingworth Reservoir, lower down and far more accessible, was graced by the title of 'Lake' and became a pleasure resort in the mid-1800s. It was also known as 'Th' Weyvers' Sayport' and thousands of visitors flocked to its shores in the days before cheap trips to the seaside. It had many pubs, open-air 'dancing stages', the all-important side-shows (including a steam-driven roundabout housed in its own building, the horses huge and brown, totally natural and undecorated), photographers offering daguerreotype prints, a steam ferry across to the pleasure garden on the southern shore, known as 'Th' Cheshire Side'. In the 1870s, indeed, the visitors were able to watch Captain Webb practising for his cross-channel swim, in what is reputed to be some of the coldest water in England! And all this set against a splendid Pennine back-drop and far above the smoke and stink of the Victorian town! Now, after a long decline, the lake is enjoying a renaissance as the nucleus of a Country Park; many of the visitors discovering the lake express surprise that such a feature should have started life as a feeder for a work-day canal.

Even the utilitarian feeder channels have their place in the landscape. The Broadhead Drain points the way from the main road to Robin Hood's Bed and provides a level route for visitors to the Roman road. The Hollingworth feeder marks a route all the way from the lake along the valley shelf to Summit. In contrast, the channel bringing water from Warland Clough to the canal (and recently restored to use by local canal enthusiasts) cuts deep into the hillside, practically engulfed by jungle-like foliage. The engineering works have weathered and merged into the landscape and become very much part of the Pennine scenery; but to stand below the massive embankment holding back the waters of Warland is to feel an intense admiration for the skill of the engineer of 1800, as well as a distinct tingle of apprehension for the safety of the massive construction!

8
'THE NORTH' BEGINS

The opening of the first trans-Pennine canal in 1804 could be said to mark the start of the Great Age—of expansion, development and progress. 'Northern' history, so inextricably tied to the nineteenth century, began with this first positive link across the Pennines.

Change was set upon change; from now on it was to be a constant process of development, innovation and invention, accelerating as the century advanced until by the end of the century the North was as positively identifiable as it has ever been. And alongside the physical development came a growing awareness of an individual character—'the North' as a cohesive unit—philosophical as well as purely physical.

Some of the changes were violent, some merely unsettling, producing an inner feeling of unease and disquiet. Since there was little alternative, the changes were accepted as inevitable. The combination of unease, disquiet, violence (and the acceptance of change as inevitable) contributed to the formation of a particular personality among inhabitants of the region. They became *Northerners*.

The towns doubled, trebled, quadrupled, reaching out to link with other towns around. A chain of towns developed between Colne and Blackburn, a tight network between Leeds, Halifax and Huddersfield. Anywhere between Bacup and Haslingden could be recognised as 'Rossendale'; the villages in the Calder, Colne and Tame valleys became linear towns, constricted and confined within the boundary walls of the hills.

By the time the expansion was complete, Lancashire and the West Riding were one gigantic factory, spinning, weaving, dyeing, bleaching, finishing, engineering, transporting and shipping. Its communications remained all-important; roads, railways, rivers and canals tied the factory and its workforce together, linking not only coal-field to mill-engine, loom to wharf, village to city, but mill-worker to seaside, chapel to chapel, business empire to business empire.

Not only the Piece Hall, but the whole of Halifax, was to disappear under a pall of smoke and soot-scented rain and was not to emerge for 150 years. Bradford became the woollen heart of the country and of the world. Manchester was 'Cottonopolis' (a precise and definitive description of its purpose and its pre-eminence).

Within a couple of generations, the North became the greatest concentration of industry and expertise the world had ever known; the Pennines were pierced and spanned and blackened by the turbulent industrial oceans to either side. But they remained, dominant and divisive, imposing their own regulation to the pattern and tempo of life. A severe winter could, did and does split the bustling empire down the middle, separating the two halves as surely as if they inhabited different continents.

The Other Canals

Soon after the Rochdale came the Huddersfield Canal, linking Manchester, Ashton and the Tame valley to the Colne valley and the Calder. It provided a shorter, less heavily locked trans-Pennine passage, but one suffering from twin disadvantages—narrow locks and the Standedge tunnel, which was the longest canal tunnel in the country and one capable of taking only a single line of boats. The Huddersfield was never as commercially viable as the Rochdale; apart from any other consideration, goods coming from Liverpool by wide barge had to be transhipped for the passage between Manchester and West Yorkshire, and since in the reverse direction a short (56ft) Calder and Hebble barge could work right through to the Mersey it was easier and more efficient to make the passage by way of the Rochdale.

The third trans-Pennine link, the Leeds and Liverpool Canal, was not fully complete until 1819, virtually on the edge of the railway era. Again, it had disadvantages. Its locks were wide, but short, incapable of taking the 74ft 'Mersey Flats', and its final route was a circuitous one which made it inadvisable for simple Lancashire—Yorkshire traffic.

Littleborough

Littleborough owes its existence to the particular combination brought about by the opening of the first trans-Pennine canal and, later, railway. Eighteenth-century maps show it as a number of separate isolated communities. Only a cluster of cottages and a church stand at the river crossing. 'Featherston' (Featherstall), Whitfield (on the hill leading to Calderbrook) and Calderbrook itself are marked as separate communities. 'Holme House' marks the site of the present day Summit.

In the *Notitia Cestrensis* of Bishop Gastrell of 1737, Littleborough was said to have a population of a little over 1,000—182 Church of England families and 4 families of Dissenters—and Bishop Gastrell's description of the local school about this time gives some idea of the scale of development in the area. (We are, after all, thinking of a vast area stretching from Blackstonedge to the edge of Rochdale.)

> Here is a school built on a piece of ground 33 yards long. The school is 14 yards long by 6 or 7 broad with 2 chambers over it for the Master' who has £5 a year given by Theo. Helliwell of Pyke House from his land at Sowerby Bridge, paid by 5 Trustees. The Master is nominated by the heirs of Helliwell of Pyke House. Ten children are taught.
>
> Mr Richard Helliwell gave £6 per annum from a rent charged on land at Walsden for the Master to teach poor children of the neighbourhood to read and write.

The trans-Pennine reference is typical. The Helliwells of Pike House, Littleborough, Lancashire, owned land at Sowerby Bridge, Yorkshire; the Hinchcliffe family of Cragg Vale, Mytholmroyd, owned an estate in Littleborough.

In about 1804, a traveller described a journey by coach from Manchester to Leeds and commented:

> When we got to Littleborough, we had to take a bye-road as there was no road through the valley. In this short round is a greater succession of natural and artificial beauties than are surveyed in so small a compass in any journey. The shaded streams of the meandering river and the artful line of the navigation are pleasant guides through this charming glen.

This and a poem written a few years later accurately describe the scenery at this extreme end of the Roch valley at this time:

> Behold the village op'ning on my sight,
> O'erlooked by mighty Blackstone on my right,
> While on my left, the rising hills display
> The variegated plumes of smiling May.
>
> Wider the landscape spreads
> O'er pastures green and flowering meads,
> While the brook in murmuring rill
> Gently glides from yonder hill.
>
> Now from this height I view the landscape o'er
> And sing of scenes un-noticed here before,
> Of a little church nesting midd the rising hills,
> Of woods and groves and rushing rills,
> Delightful mansions and gardens gay
> Enrobed in all the pride of smiling May.

The 'little church nesting midd the rising hills' had existed by the river crossing from 1471 and the Vicar of Rochdale noted in 1800 that, 'The chapel is in the most wretched of conditions that can be conceived, and it is a danger to the people', and even though Nonconformism had been established at Calderbrook as early as the 1750s, it was not until 1809 that the first Dissenters' chapel (known by the delightful name of 'The Methodical Piazza') was built just across the river from the decrepit old church. At the time this was an ideal situation, but in the event the Manchester & Leeds railway viaduct was built almost on top of the chapel. Within ten years of the arrival of the railway the building was described as 'little used' and it was closed in 1861; the noise of the trains overhead drowned the services in the chapel. The structure survived until 1950 when a municipal brainstorm resulted in its demolition!

The village began to expand immediately after the canal opened and a new parish church was planned and eventually opened in 1820. Although contemporary with the 'million churches' built with money demanded in reparations after the Napoleonic Wars, Holy Trinity was not one of them. It was built some yards to the north of the old 'chapel' and was described as 'a painfully plain oblong building with galleries on three sides and seating for 401 people'.

Around this time, some major improvements were made to the main Rochdale–Halifax turnpike; presumably an indication of the increased traffic using the trans-Pennine roads. 'New Road' was built parallel to the existing route but passing on the opposite side of Stubley Old Hall, and a new approach was made to the centre of the village. The old road had swung north, between the Falcon Inn and its coach house; the new route passed along the 'back' of the pub (which became the front!) and arrived at the river crossing by way of the land cleared by the demolition of the old church. Some sections of this old road still remain and it is quite apparent, even now, that the old Market Place, the centre of the village at that time, was enclosed by the inn, its coach-house and Lodge Street (the pre-Calderbrook turnpike track to Todmorden).

With two- and three-storey weavers' cottages at intervals on the road linking the village centre to the Calderbrook Turnpike junction toll-house, a canal wharf and warehouse, a new church on one side of the river and the Dissenters' chapel on the other, it was obvious that the tiny settlement was beginning to take on the appearance of a recognisable village.

Todmorden

In Todmorden, the pattern was different. The hamlets on the valley shelf existed, and most people lived in them, rather than in the valley bottom. But a degree of building had taken place around the church and the meeting of the rivers and valley roads. A meeting was held in Todmorden in 1801 with a view to setting up a market, and the following year the market was established. By this time the 'centre' of Todmorden already had about forty cottages, some small shops, the old Todmorden Hall, St Mary's Church and two or three inns. Development here was a more natural progression and between 1801 and 1811 the population increased from 2,515 to 3,652. By 1814 coaching had begun and Todmorden had a parson, a doctor, six grocers, three butchers, six pubs and a handful of mills, including one specifically described as a 'steam' factory. This was the mill of Henry Ramsbottom at Salford—a significant site that was developed immediately after the canal was opened. Here, too, there were wharves and warehouses and a mile or so nearer Walsden was (and is) the splendid Gauxholme canal warehouse, a notable example of the type.

The various Nonconformist sects had (literally) set up house in many dwellings in the area during the second half of the eighteenth century; the rapidly increasing population made it possible for them to start building special chapels. In 1807 the Quakers moved to larger premises and in the same year the Independents built themselves a place of worship. In 1818 it was the Baptists, then the Methodists, then the Wesleyans. Finally, in 1828 came agitation for a new St Mary's Church. Cross Stone Church had been rebuilt, using finance drawn from France after the Napoleonic Wars.

Todmorden was, therefore, much more of a town than Littleborough. The Fielden family had been well-established locally for many years and would seem to have 'pulled together' the various strands to form a substantial settlement. By 1815 Todmorden had its own Folly (a rare edifice hereabouts) in Stoodley Pike. Although a pike (probably the site of a beacon fire) had existed earlier, a 120ft high monument was raised on top of the 1,300ft ridge south-east of the town. It was erected to commemorate the Peace of Ghent in 1814 and was completed after the Battle of Waterloo in 1815. However, on the day the Crimean War was declared in 1854 it collapsed. It was rebuilt in 1856 and survived the start and finish of the Boer War and the beginning of World War I. However, on the morning of 11 November 1918 it collapsed! It has been watched closely on a number of occasions since that time but has not yet shown signs of even a slight tilt!

The turnpike trusts carried out various road improvements in Todmorden during the early years of the nineteenth century. In 1807, for instance, it was decided to 'set' (pave) a section of road from the canal bridge to Pickles Bridge and this stretch of road is still known locally as 'Pavement'.

Todmorden, of course, was in a curious position, with the Lancashire—Yorkshire boundary running directly through the middle of the 'town'. It had, in effect, two toll-bars, for Lancashire and Yorkshire respectively, each with its own toll-keeper.

In 1824 there was a major road improvement. A new turnpike

was built between the centre of Littleborough and Steanor-bottom, as the building of the canal had drained the valley floor to such an extent that building a road was possible. Toll-houses were, of course, built at either end of this new road and both still exist. The toll-bar at the Littleborough end controlled both the old Halifax and new Todmorden turnpike roads, and the one at Steanorbottom was a replacement for a previous building just a little way up the Calderbrook turnpike at Dog Isles, Deanhead—which had been on the junction of the Reddyshore Scoutgate and the (then) new Calderbrook road.

The Steanorbottom toll-house was of a classic type—semi-hexagonal with some pretensions to architectural styling. The windows were semi-circular headed, the central door had a crude pediment and the tariff board was housed in a semi-circular headed recess above. It was lived in for some time after it ceased duty as a toll-house but was derelict for many years. Then in 1972 a storm dislodged some of the roofing slabs and they, in turn, brought down some of the stones. There was immediate talk of shipping the building away and re-erecting it in the Castle Museum in York, and the tariff board was, in fact, removed, but it was finally decided to restore the toll-house on site.

Stage-coaches

The new turnpike road soon saw a regular stage-coach service. John Crossley of Scaitcliffe, Todmorden, and some fellow townspeople raised £500 to persuade a proprietor to run coaches from Manchester to Halifax by way of Todmorden and the Calder valley. The proprietor of the Golden Lion Inn, Tod-morden, was one of the promoters of the service; the inn became one of the stages and a post office was opened there.

At first the service ran on Tuesdays and Fridays and later the coach was joined by the *Shuttle* and the *Perseverance*. The latter left Halifax every day at 7am, except on Tuesday when it departed at 6am. Tuesday was the day of the Manchester Cotton Market and the whole service was much used by the local merchants. The fare from Rochdale to Manchester was 6/-, which was a prodigious sum in those days; so it is not surprising that many local business men still did the journey on horseback.

Even though the new road up the valley from Littleborough was built on land drained by the construction of the canal, there was little development at the village end until well on into the nineteenth century. The 'meandering river' noted by the traveller of 1804 could become a raging torrent in a matter of hours and the substantially level area immediately to the north of the village was regularly inundated. Only where the road began to rise was it considered wise to build and it was here that Laurence Newall, gentleman landowner and a member of the prominent local family, built the Gale Inn and a cotton-spinning mill alongside. This was a mill in the modern manner—steam driven and well away from both river and canal.

Laurence Newall had been one of the subscribers to the new church in Littleborough and had requested that his money be spent in such a way that he could see what he had given. The church has a spire—unusual in this area at the time—which can be seen quite clearly across the flat land from Newall's home at Townhouse!

'Gale' itself refers to the sweet myrtle that grew in the locality. Its leaves were used in wool-dyeing and it was found that if the berries and leaves were steeped in ale the drink became significantly more powerful. It was probably for this reason that the 'Blooming Gale Lodge' which used to meet at the Gale Inn used the plant as its emblem.

The developments along the new road were most noticeable at Summit. Before 1800 it was a natural, well-wooded clough with a stream of clear water running through it. The building of the canal began the desecration. Chelburn Wood disappeared when the reservoirs were built in the valley there and gradually the others were cut down until they remained only in place-names: 'Sladen Wood', 'Grove' and 'Timbercliffe'.

Summit

A concentration of weavers' cottages appeared along the road near its highest point and many footpaths and lanes linked this settlement to the older one at Calderbrook on the hill above. 'Summit' as a place had not yet become accepted. It was a natural extension of Calderbrook down to the new road and the linking paths were clearly heavily used.

Once again, Nonconformism was a feature of this outlying district. Methodism had been brought into the area by William Grimshaw in 1749 and house meetings developed. As the community grew, a Wesleyan Chapel was built at Smithy Nook in 1817 and given the evocative name of 'Mount Gilead'. Then, in the year the road opened, the Reverend John Ely of Providence Chapel and a supporter of the 'Cookite' breakaway movement of Congregationalists came to Summit and was instrumental in setting up a meeting at a house just below the Summit Inn. A few years later Ely persuaded a newly ordained minister, Henry Cheetham, to take over the Summit group and they opened their splendidly named 'Summit Ebenezer Congregational' chapel in 1834. By this time the Methodists, too, were a large enough group to contemplate building their own chapel, which they did in 1839, naming it 'Temple'. Finally, in 1866, the dissident Primitive Methodists built their own chapel on the 'new' road just between the first Methodist chapel and the Congregationalists.

So, with a population not much in excess of 1,500, the settlement at the northern end of the valley developed four thunderously named chapels ('Mount Gilead', 'Ebenezer', 'Temple' and 'Summit Primitive') within the space of fifty years and three of them within barely twenty years. Significantly, the early links with Todmorden were retained and, even now, the Summit Primitive Methodist Chapel comes within the Todmorden circuit rather than the Littleborough one. Equally significantly, perhaps, these chapels were all built and were exerting their influence to its ultimate before the first Church of England building in the area was built. St James', Calderbrook, was not built until 1872 and was only the second church to be built in an area which had first had a church 400 years before. By the time this church was built, no less then sixteen Nonconformist chapels had been built and one—the Methodical Piazza—had actually already closed.

The Blackstonedge New Road

The turnpike roads were an indispensable part of the economy of the region. Canals provided efficient bulk transport, but there

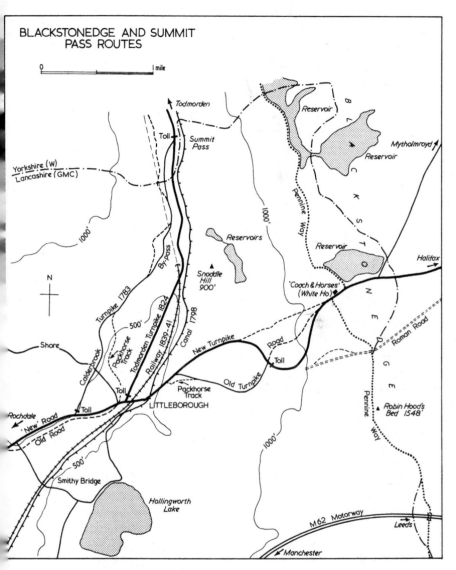

BLACKSTONEDGE AND SUMMIT
PASS ROUTES

was still a need for further improvements to the inadequate
trans-Pennine roads. The Blackstonedge road, for instance, the
'Exceeding deep and ruinous' road of the Parliamentary petition
of 1734, was turnpiked and improved in various ways, but it was
obvious towards the end of the century that it was no longer suitable for the greatly increased traffic using it. Stage-coaches had

particular difficulty as shortly after leaving Littleborough they faced the steep hill up from Durn to Gatehouse and, even though the gradient had been somewhat eased by the excavation of a substantial cutting at the top of the hill, coaches had to take on extra horses at the Rake Inn.

The exact line of the road was not described in the petition of 1734 and the Third Blackstonedge Turnpike Trust Act of 1765 is concerned mainly with the general detail of the road running from the Market Cross in Rochdale to its counterpart in Halifax. However, there is a drawing of the then New road in Kitchen's *Post Chaise Companion Through England and Wales*, published in 1767, and the first Manchester Directory indicates that there was a coach service over Blackstonedge. In 1772 this was weekly, but in 1781 it was a daily service.

Gradually an entirely new road up the steep western slope of Blackstonedge took shape. It took an easier route from the Rake Inn, crossing an embankment over the Lydgate Clough valley (massive by the standards of the time), curving round the northern flank of Stormer Hill to cross the old road (conveniently for the Turnpike Trust) at the already established Stormer Bar toll-house. At this point the road was actually heading away from its ultimate destination, the White House at the top of the edge, but it was carefully graded to run round in a wide arc, clipping the end of the Roman road and then rising on a relatively even gradient up the shoulder of the ridge. Once the new road was fully open, the section of the old route 'above' Stormer Bar was abandoned.

Some of the massively-hewn guide posts for this 'new' road still exist on the unfenced section between Stormer Bar and the White House Inn. An Act of 1795 ordered the erection of such posts along turnpike roads and, although the first reliable details of the road do not emerge until the 1844 Ordnance Survey, it is suggested that the whole road was complete by 1820.

With the turnpike roads over Blackstonedge and up the valley to Todmorden established and the canal open, Littleborough, which had so recently been merely a cluster of cottages by the river crossing, became the kingpin for the routes across the Pennines. By 1821, about fifteen coaches were using the Blackstonedge route, including the Royal Mail to York and the *Defiance* to

(*above*) The White House 'Coach and Horses Inn', Blackstonedge. Just below the crest of Blackstonedge, the inn is visible from many miles away. Even at this date (about 1880) it was whitewashed. The stone wall to the right marks the boundary of the Rochdale Canal Company's land and the embankment of Blackstonedge Reservoir is visible behind the inn. Just visible on the left is the track and feeder channel leading off to White Holme, Warland and Light Hazzles reservoirs. (*below*) Halifax Piece Hall. The Piece Hall was opened in 1779 and it was here that the hand-loom weavers brought their 'pieces' for sale to the merchants. The central courtyard of the Hall measures approximately 110yd × 91yd and there are some 315 rooms opening off the galleries, each one originally rented at £28 per year. The smaller weavers showed off their cuts in the central area. The Hall has been recently restored and is now a thriving craft centre and museum. Regular markets (as here) are also held. The spire in the background is the 'Square' Congregational Church built in 1856–7. The church was built largely thanks to the efforts of the Crossley family; it replaced an earlier structure of 1772 which then became the Sunday School

The upper Roch valley shortly after the opening of the Manchester & Leeds Railway. From left to right, the canal, the railway and the Todmorden turnpike (built after the coming of the canal had drained the marshy valley-bottom). To the left of the church in the background is the Halifax turnpike, to the right the road leading to Rochdale. The line of trees (*left centre*) marks the old road leading from the village to the Calderbrook turnpike. At this date the 'town' of Littleborough was still a cluster of cottages and a church close by the river crossing, but the first steam-powered mills have been built – at Gale (*centre*) and Grove (*right*). Brindley's alternative line for the canal would have brought it along the northern (*right hand*) side of the valley, round the hill at Gale to join the line as built just to the right of the viewpoint. The 'alternative' Bury proposal would have brought the canal round the hill, across the valley and off into Lydgate valley below the viewpoint to the left

Hebden Bridge

Leeds. After 1826 they were joined by the coaches running to and from Manchester and Halifax via Todmorden (*Shuttle* and *Perseverance* and so on) and by 1830, on the threshold of the railway era, there were added the *Old* and *New York* coaches, the *High Flyer*, the *Duke of Leeds* and the *Commerce*.

With water power in abundance, coal for the digging just beneath the surface, steam engines making their appearance in the new mills, the turnpike roads and the canals bringing raw materials into and taking finished goods out of the area, the Pennines were beginning to present a very different face to the world. Significantly perhaps, Coalbrookdale, down in Shropshire, where the Industrial Revolution had started, was already in decline by this time. In 1825, the Stockton & Darlington Railway opened, heralding an entirely new era, and in the same year it was suggested that if a trans-Pennine railway could be built the easiest route would be by way of the Roch valley and Calderdale. The new turnpikes were only a handful of years old and even the 'artful line of the navigation' a mere twenty-five.

9
WITH AND WITHOUT
THE BRONTËS

The new roads may have spanned the Pennines and the canals brought new developments in the valleys, but the real prosperity still lay rooted in the upland villages where the staunchly independent hand-loom weavers held sway.

Heptonstall and Luddenden, Sowerby, Mankinholes and Calderbrook, Dobcross, Diggle and Delph, Haworth, Ripponden and the Colne valley; it was here that the expertise lay. The Fielden Brothers of Waterside, Todmorden, were powers to be reckoned with, but the strength of their empire lay in the army of weavers spinning their thread. The weavers of both Summit and Smithy Nook, Calderbrook, were supplied with their raw materials by Fielden's and then sold back so that the same firm could dispose of the finished product. Hand-loom weaving was considered to be a 'good' trade right up to the late 1830s.

It was to one of these upland villages that the Reverend Patrick Brontë brought his ailing wife and six young children in 1821. His arrival was not altogether uneventful. After the death of the famous William Grimshaw, the living had passed to a John Richardson and then to a James Charnock. The old, fervent fires of Methodism still crackled away and Haworth still asserted its resolute independence from time to time. The Church authorities in Bradford appointed Brontë to the living without consulting the local parishioners. This fact was pointed out (presumably rather firmly) to Mr Brontë and he promptly withdrew from the post. The Church authorities then appointed the Reverend Samuel Redhead who had served as curate under Charnock, again without consulting the Haworth people but presumably assuming that he would be acceptable.

He was not, and the parishioners of St Michael's took devastating revenge. Redhead had a full church for his first service, but as the reading of the First Lesson began the congregation walked out. The following Sunday the church was again full, the congregation quiet. Then a man rode into the church mounted on a donkey. Pandemonium broke out and the Reverend Samuel Redhead retired. On the third Sunday the congregation brought a drunken chimney-sweep into the church with them. The vicar tried to read the service, but in the middle of his sermon the sweep clambered into the pulpit, flung his arms round Redhead and kissed him. Redhead tried to leave the church but was held by the crowd, pushed down the aisle and hurled into a pile of soot left outside the church door by the sweep. Eventually he escaped to the 'Black Bull'.

Patrick Brontë

Patrick Brontë then returned, this time at the invitation of the Haworth parishioners. Many years later Redhead, too, returned, at Brontë's invitation. He was received warmly by the populace who listened to him attentively. But they told him in no uncertain terms that they would stone him, if necessary, in order to maintain their rights.

Far from being a remote and uncivilised hill-top hamlet in the wilds of Yorkshire, Haworth was a thriving industrial centre with a radical frame of mind ruthlessly and resolutely up-to-date. It is estimated that there were upwards of 1,000 hand-loom weavers within five miles of Haworth and by the time Brontë arrived a half-dozen of the mills were equipped with steam-engines. The village itself was about three times the size it is now.

There were about three times as many people living in the area as there are now, and in the village at least, conditions were appalling. The mortality was said to be higher than in the slums of Manchester or Liverpool and one of the drinking water sources welled up inside the churchyard itself.

Very soon after the family arrived in Haworth, Mrs Brontë died. Mr Brontë looked around for a new wife, and, after the manner of the time, proposed to a lady he had previously been acquainted with. She declined the honour and eventually Patrick Brontë persuaded his late wife's sister to join him in Haworth as his housekeeper. Meanwhile, the children had been sent away to a school for the daughters of clergymen in the Lake District and it was here that the two eldest girls, Maria and Elizabeth, tragically died, leaving the nine-year-old Charlotte as the eldest child. Brontë immediately brought the children back to Haworth.

Behind the Facade

The image of the Brontës is very much that of three maidenly sisters shut away in a mist-shrouded parsonage with a drug-ridden brother, writing and coughing their ways to early graves. In fact no one died at Haworth parsonage for twenty-five years, and if the house was cold and bleak it was mainly because the Reverend Patrick Brontë had a pathological fear of fire and refused to have either curtains or floor coverings in the rooms.

All the family were writers. Brontë himself had published poetry and a novel during the years 1811–15 and Branwell also wrote. It has recently been suggested that it was Branwell who really 'ghosted' *Wuthering Heights* for Emily, which is a theory that must surely shock the purists!

Living as they did in this rip-roaring 'new' town, exposed to all its trials and joys (as vicars' families often are) with a tearaway young brother and with plenty of time on their hands and devastating talent at their finger-tips, it is perhaps less surprising that they wrote as they did.

And write they did! It is estimated that Charlotte, Emily and Anne wrote more before they were thirteen years old than afterwards. These were complicated, contrived sagas, written in tiny handwriting in books of postage-stamp size. Then came poetry. Charlotte discovered that Emily had written poetry secretly and, apparently, a monumental row ensued. Later, the sisters published, at their own expense, a collection of poetry. Copies were sent to Wordsworth and Southey, but few, if any, copies were actually sold.

Charlotte, Emily and Anne Brontë became Currer, Ellis and Acton Bell (on reflection curiously asexual names) and continued writing—Charlotte *The Professor*, Emily *Wuthering Heights* and Anne *Agnes Gray*. Thirteen publishers were approached before, probably to Charlotte's chagrin, *Wuthering Heights* and *Agnes Gray* were accepted for publication. Charlotte was advised to write a 'popular' novel. Patrick Brontë

Haworth Parsonage

was advised to have an operation on his eyes and took Charlotte with him to Manchester, to nurse him after his operation. It was here, not in Haworth, that she wrote *Jane Eyre*.

They may have travelled by train; the line was open from Manchester to Hebden Bridge and Leeds by then and, in fact, Branwell worked as a ticket clerk at Luddendenfoot for a short time. (When he left it is said the books did not quite balance!)

Charlotte sent the manuscript of *Jane Eyre* off to a publisher and he took it home, to dip into it in an exploratory way. In the event he read it at one sitting and accepted it immediately. Then, in one short, saddening year Emily, Anne and Branwell died and 1847 saw Charlotte alone at the parsonage with the ageing Patrick.

And yet, she was not alone. She was a highly successful author with an income of £1,500 a year. She was visited by that other redoubtable author, Elizabeth Gaskell, and received a proposal from Arthur Bell Nicholls, her father's curate. Patrick Brontë now asserted his authority. Charlotte had £1,500 a year and Nicholls had £40. Prophetically he warned Charlotte that if she, at thirty-eight, married, she would be dead within the year. And he sacked Nicholls. Charlotte defied him, married, and was indeed dead (in the early stages of pregnancy) within a year. The brief and glittering, yet poignant, story was over.

Haworth now seethes with visitors; upwards of 700,000 people fill the steep Main Street every year, crowd the church-yard and tramp dutifully through the parsonage.

The Influences

It is said that Charlotte, Emily and Anne Brontë were the right people in the right place at the right time and presumably this de-scription is not meant to denigrate them. But a placid phrase of this sort does not quite describe their achievement. Much of the work is mundane—particularly by present-day standards—and they seem to have stayed well away from the contemporary Haworth scene of the 1840s, even though they lived among the sturdily independent (and, by the 1840s redundant, and desper-ate) weavers of Haworth. Hardly ever does a philosophy surface, a theory germinate.

Yet the ambience is there. Just beneath the surface of each book the conscious 'reality' is stirring. Top Withens Farm exists and, just as surely, 'Wuthering Heights' exists. Everything that makes up the complicated mentality—and physicality—of the moorland setting has been absorbed, distilled and set down dra-matically. But nothing has been invented.

The atmosphere the Brontës created is as accurate as any; far more accurate an atmosphere than that of the Northern working-class areas created by the New Wave of the 1950s and 60s. Factually, the Brontës are inferior to Mrs Gaskell, but envi-ronmentally, they are supreme. To stand on any moor-top is to sense the isolation and the loneliness, and, more than that, to feel some distant secret creeping in. Dark legends are all around and are bedded deep in the soul, swirling around the mind as the mist swirls across the moor. The Brontës reacted to all this in a specific, yet almost indefinable way.

90

10
ROUGH MEN, ROUGH TIMES
AND IRON ROADS

Colliery railways (more correctly 'tram-roads') had developed to a considerable extent by the time the first passenger railways were conceived; coal was brought by short, horse-drawn lines to the Leeds and Liverpool Canal in the Wigan area and one of the earliest such lines was from Pewfall Colliery to the Sankey Canal, opened in about 1766.

There were a few examples in the South Pennine area, (notably the tramway from Tunshill colliery down to Hollingworth Lake) but in the main coal was simply dug out and used locally. In the Littleborough area, for instance, where coal was readily available just below the surface, it is estimated that there were 300 coal workings; Clegg's Mill at Shore, Littleborough, mined its own coal in workings on the moor just above the mill. Few of these Pennine workings were mines in the accepted term. They were 'Breast 'Ees' (breast high) or 'Light Hole' pits—drift-workings cut into the side of the hill.

There are many sites still remaining, but one of the easiest to appreciate is the Cleggswood colliery close by the station at Littleborough. Here both coal and clay were mined and there was a rope-hauled plateway ('L' section rails laid to take wagons with flat rather than flanged wheels) leading down from the colliery mouth to a wharf on the Rochdale Canal. The sough or drainage channel for this mine cut right through the hill to appear in the Ealees valley just below the present Hollingworth Lake Country Park Information Centre.

There was mining in the Ealees valley too, and in Lydgate Clough to the north (and, in between, the substantial Gatehouse colliery). The Lydgate workings were of the most basic kind—simple holes driven into the hillside—but the remains show a drainage channel cut down the centre of the wagon track leading from the workings. Coal working hereabouts was only marginally economic (although the Lydgate mines were reopened during the 1926 General Strike) and where the Pennine grit-

91

stone pushed up through the coal-measures the field petered out anyway. Most of the locally mined coal was of poor quality and although colliery working continued (for instance at Butterworth Hall, Milnrow) until relatively recently, most coal, and specifically better-quality coal, was brought into the developing Pennine area by the canals.

In 1803, a plateway was built to connect the two halves of the Lancaster Canal after the original plan to link Walton Summit, near Chorley, to Preston by a water-way had been abandoned on the grounds of cost. There were several sharp inclines on this line and the trains of wagons were pulled up by means of a traction rope and stationary steam engine sited at the top of the hill. This system was also used on the Bolton & Leigh Railway, opened in 1828, three years after the opening of the Stockton & Darlington Railway, the first accepted 'public' railway. The Bolton & Leigh used edge-rail and wagons with flanged wheels, and was standard gauge. The rails were laid on stone blocks.

Nearer to the Pennines, a proposal was made to link Manchester and Bolton by railway. The Manchester, Bolton and Bury Canal had been opened in 1797 and had received a proposal from the Leeds and Liverpool Canal that it should be linked to their canal. So the Manchester, Bolton and Bury was converted to 'broad' canal specifications at considerable expense, to bring it up to the standards of the Leeds and Liverpool. However, nothing came of the proposals and, by 1828, with the railway between Bolton and Leigh open, the future of the canal was, to say the least, uncertain. An Act of Parliament to convert the canal to a railway received the assent on 23 August 1831 (less than a year after the opening of the Liverpool & Manchester Railway) but subsequently the engineer appointed to carry out a survey advised that the canal should be retained and the railway built alongside. Work began in 1833 and the line was opened in 1838.

Manchester to Leeds

However, the promoters of a railway between Manchester and Leeds were by no means idle. A first proposal in 1825 had clearly been premature, but by 1830, with the Liverpool & Manchester

Railway approaching completion, they invited George Stephenson to survey a line between the two cities. His report was presented on 15 November 1830, only a few weeks after the opening of the Liverpool & Manchester Railway, the first public passenger railway.

In his report Stephenson suggested that the Leeds line should start from the existing Liverpool Road station in Manchester and had this early proposal been adopted as a principle, British cities would have been spared the plethora of separate stations owned by different companies. At the height of the railway age, Manchester had five separate railway stations: the Lancashire & Yorkshire at Victoria; the London & North Western at Exchange; the Midland at Central; the oddly ambivalent 'Mayfield'; and the LNWR and Great Central running the two sides of London Road. The Manchester, South Junction and Altrincham line also used London Road and the Cheshire Lines Committee also used Central. The Midland, LNWR and Great Central offered competing routes to London—two of them from the joint station which became Piccadilly. Even the Great Northern, which had little, if any, connection with the Manchester area, nevertheless maintained a goods station hard alongside Central station.

If Stephenson had had his way, Manchester might have developed one joint station, and this idea was revived as late as the immediate post-war period. Redevelopment plans published at that time showed a large station on the site of the now-redundant Exchange.

As his assistant, Stephenson had appointed Thomas Gooch, who was the bearer of a surname famous in railway circles. His brother John became locomotive engineer to the London & South Western Railway and Daniel, another brother, was to become the great locomotive engineer and Chairman of the GWR. Gooch had to work against the clock to carry out the survey in time for its submission to Parliament and it is said that the last levels were taken by torchlight at the summit level of the Rochdale Canal and the necessary documents rushed by fast carriage, specially hired, to be lodged with the Clerks of the Peace at Wakefield and Preston at the last possible minute.

The First Application

The Bill was introduced to Parliament on 28 February 1831 but after its Second Reading it was delayed by opposition from the Rochdale Canal Company, Parliament was dissolved shortly afterwards and the Bill was lost. The Canal Company insisted that it could deliver goods from Manchester to Halifax in twenty hours at a rate of 2d per ton mile. It also insisted that speed was **not the first** essential and pointed out that half its income was derived from the transport of grain and about a quarter from stone flags. The railway company replied that if the information supplied by the canal company was correct they need not fear competition! They pointed out that they could do the journey from Manchester to Halifax in two to three hours.

The Bill was reintroduced in June and got as far as the Committee Stage before it was, once again, thrown out. History seemed to be repeating itself, but this time with the canal company as a major objector.

More important historical hazards, in the shape of the Reform Act of 1832, now intervened and it was not until 1835 that another attempt to build the railway was made. At a meeting in Manchester the company was reconstituted, Stephenson was once again brought in as engineer and a new development plan was drawn up.

The route envisaged included provisions for three tunnels, one of 1,705yd at the summit level and two others of 126yd and 180yd approximately. Beyond Sowerby Bridge the line was to run alongside the Calder and through Wakefield. The plan then was for the line to join the proposed North Midland railway to Leeds near Normanton.

A Bill was introduced into Parliament in February 1836 and, once again, the Rochdale Canal Company was among the objectors. The company gave many reasons why railways should not be introduced into the area. In stating one of its objections, it declared:

> The great public advantage offered by the Rochdale Canal, the serious investment upon that undertaking and the small return, not 2½% hitherto yielded to the Company give them the most genuine hope that Parliament will, by rejecting the Railway Bill leave them in undisturbed possession of their property.

Assent

Parliament did not agree, and the Bill received the Royal Assent on 4 July 1836. The Act authorised a joint stock capital of £1,300,000 and an additional £433,000 by loan. Some final adjustments to the proposed route were required and were agreed by November. An Act of 5 May 1837 authorised the line and construction began on 18 August. The line was now to begin at Oldham Road, Manchester, rather than the Liverpool Road station; however, only four years after the line first opened, it was linked to the Liverpool & Manchester by way of the new Victoria station. In fact, the fate of Oldham Road station was sealed before it even opened; the site for the Victoria station was purchased in August 1838.

Recognising that the Summit tunnel would be a major engineering work, Thomas Gooch (appointed as Stephenson's assistant again) authorised the sinking of the first working shaft in January 1838, but work on the driftway did not go well and in March 1839, when the completed railway was rapidly approaching Littleborough, Gooch, his patience exhausted, replaced the original contractors, Evans and Copeland, with John Stephenson. (He was no relation to George, but a man whose first work had been on the Stockton & Darlington and one who was to go on to become one of the major railway engineers.)

Unrest

The tunnel was a prodigious achievement. At 2,885yd, it was the longest yet constructed and contained 23 million bricks and 8,000 tons of cement. The northern mouth is 331ft above the level of the old Oldham Road station and the tunnel is on a 1 in 130 gradient falling to the south. If the statistics are impressive, the story of the building of the tunnel is equally dramatic. Naturally there was considerable loss of life, but there was also an attempt to form a 'combination' to represent the men's grievances. There was much labour agitation locally at the time. An early Chartist meeting at Kersal Moor in Salford attracted 50,000 people and in March 1839 (the same month in which Gooch replaced Evans and Copeland by John Stephenson) the *Bolton Free Press* reported that there was 'extensive speculation in the Pike trade'. Common halberds were fetching 9d to 1/3d and those with 'a sharp-edged hook for cutting horses' girths' as much as 2/9d.

In August of that year Parliament rejected a petition for the six principles brought by the Chartists, but the month of strikes that was due to follow failed entirely. Many Chartist leaders were arrested and others fled. During searches by the authorities in Bury, eighteen pikes and a quantity of musket balls were found hidden under the floor of the Mechanics' Hall. On 20 September the *Bolton Free Press* reported that the cause of Chartism was dead and that 'a great many deadly weapons' had been sold as old iron.

Undoubtedly the men working on the Summit tunnel were influenced by the unrest apparent locally. The combination was formed among bricklayers (who, in fact, were highly paid at 6/6d a ten-hour day) and subsequently several of them appeared before the Rochdale magistrates and were sentenced to three months' imprisonment.

Truck System

One of the outstanding grievances was the Truck system which operated widely in the growing industrial areas. It was certainly not uncommon for a shop selling basic goods to be attached to a mill or warehouse and the workpeople to be obliged to buy their goods from the shop. In 1842, for instance, Dr P. M. McDouall of Ramsbottom told the Select Committee on the Payment of Wages that in his area, between Manchester and Haslingden, he knew of only one firm which was not involved in the Truck system. He reported:

> I saw a person a fortnight ago who received 3d for a week's wages in consequence of a deduction for clothing ... I have known of one case of 1½d being paid ... the men are constantly assailed by the Masters to know where they bought their clothing.

McDouall also described to the committee how people employed by Grants of Ramsbottom were given a wage ticket which they had to take to a public house owned by the firm. The landlord changed the ticket for them, but only after deducting threepence for each person which they had to take in drink. When a member of the Committee asked what would happen if a man insisted on being given his threepence instead of drink, McDouall replied: 'There would be a complaint made regarding him, and it would be easy to find fault with his work.'

The Grants of Ramsbottom were Charles Dickens' Cheeryble Brothers, and theirs was by no means the most insidious example of the system, but with the combination of the Truck system, the harsh working conditions and the fiery temperament of the navvies, it is surprising that there was so little trouble during the building of the railway. It has recently been suggested that as a reaction to the Truck system, an early form of Co-op was set up by the workers on the tunnel. Certainly the Pioneers in Rochdale followed only a few years after the work on the tunnel was in progress; Rochdale is five miles or so from the tunnel-mouth and many men who worked on the railway settled locally and were influential in various ways.

The last brick was keyed into place on 11 December 1840, some months after the first sections of the railway to either side were opened. The Manchester–Littleborough section had opened with some considerable flourish on 3 July 1839 and the line from Normanton up the Calder valley to Hebden Bridge opened early in October 1840. Passengers bridged the gap between the railheads by carriage.

The Tunnels

There were many heavy engineering works on the section of the line between Littleborough and Hebden Bridge, and one of them, a proposed tunnel at Charlestown, near the Hebble End of canal fame, proved well-nigh insuperable. Originally, Gooch had intended a tunnel here, 250yd long and 50ft deep, penetrating a spur of the hillside. But the loose, unstable earth gave trouble from the start and in June 1840, eighteen months after the contract had been first let, it was reported that the masonry inside the tunnel was collapsing. Reluctantly, the tunnel was abandoned and the line taken round the obstacle. The decided kink in the line is still apparent today.

Apart from the great Summit tunnel and the abandoned one at

Summit Tunnel West. With the only known example of the coat of arms of the Manchester & Leeds Railway. Dated 1839. The main tunnel entrance is immediately beyond

Charlestown, there were six other tunnels in the nine miles between Littleborough and Hebden Bridge. Deanroyd (70yd) is virtually part of Summit tunnel, separated from it by a great oval shaft. Then comes Winterbutlee (306yd). Then, between Todmorden and Hebden Bridge are three short tunnels in quick succession: Millwood (225yd); Castle Hill (194yd); Horsfall (274yd); and finally Weasal Hall (109yd). Summit West (41yd), where the Littleborough–Todmorden road crosses the

98

railway, is officially a tunnel and it was on the portico that the company placed its coat of arms. This still remains, the only known remaining example of the crest of the Manchester & Leeds Railway.

In addition to the tunnels, there were two major viaducts to construct on this extremely difficult trans-Pennine section, the long Gauxholme viaduct between Walsden and Todmorden and the impressive structure carrying the line across the town centre of Todmorden itself. There were other viaducts too, notably at Charlestown, where the railway changed from the north to the south side of the valley, crossing road, river and canal in one leap. So it is not surprising that the opening of this section of the line was delayed some twenty months after that first section between Manchester and Littleborough.

A plaque on the present Littleborough station commemorates the start of the first stage of the trans-Pennine railway journey, when the first train left Manchester at noon. The train consisted of eleven carriages hauled by two 0–4–2 locomotives, *Stephenson* and *Kenyon*. It was followed shortly afterwards by a second train pulled by two similar engines, *Stanley* and *Lancaster*. On the ceremonial runs, the trains travelled as far as the tunnel mouth and on the following day when the public service started between Manchester and Littleborough, 3,100 people were carried. The fares for the 14 mile journey were First Class 4/-, Second Class 2/6d and Third Class 1/6d. Private carriages were also conveyed on flat wagons and the charge for these was 6d per mile for two-wheeled carriages and 9d per mile for those with four.

The Completed Railway

Finally, in March 1841, the tunnel was completed and the line opened throughout. George Stephenson visited the tunnel and was well satisfied with what he saw. 'I will stake my character and my head,' he is reported as saying, 'if that tunnel ever give way, so as to cause danger to the public passing through it. Taking it as a whole, I don't think there is such another piece of work in the world.'

The first carriages were, naturally, four-wheeled vehicles.

First Class had three compartments, upholstered seats and sash windows, and were painted blue. The Second Class carriages also had three compartments but were shorter, making the space between the seats rather too narrow for comfort. In place of glass they had yellow wooden shutters. Third Class passengers were carried in open wagons and a description of a journey on the Manchester & Leeds Railway in one of these vehicles is enlightening:

> The third class carriages were big boxes, without seats and neck-high. Children and people of small stature were Monarchs of all they surveyed, and that was limited to the contents of the big box and the sky overhead. There were holes at the bottom of the box to let off rain water unabsorbed by people's clothes, open umbrellas being an unendurable nuisance. Having thus passed through various tunnels pouring down floods of dirty water and behind a steam engine belching forth volumes of black smoke and showers of hot ashes, these heroic passengers, after an hour and three quarters in purgatory, safely arrived at their destination, but so wet, bedraggled and begrimed that they had first to recognise the anxious friends who met them, for their friends knew not them who had been metamorphized from whites to blacks during their exciting and perilous journey.

For all its peril and excitement, the Manchester & Leeds was an outstanding achievement. It had an early form of signalling and was the first to introduce the printed ticket. Thomas Edmondson who had invented a machine for printing tickets had demonstrated it to his employers, the Newcastle & Carlisle Railway, and, finding them uninterested in his invention, approached the Manchester & Leeds. For them, he devised a series of special tickets. Those for passengers going in the Yorkshire direction had a fleece printed on the back and those travelling into Lancashire had a bale of cotton. First Class tickets had plain backs, Second Class had horizontal lines, Third Class horizontal and vertical lines. Thus any unauthorised addition to the ticket reduced its value, rather than enhanced it. The obvious advantages of this system were immediately recognised and it was soon adopted as a standard form of railway ticket. Some of the familiar machines for dating these tickets have only just disappeared from British Rail stations.

The M & L Today

A surprising amount of the Manchester & Leeds Railway remains. The tunnels, viaducts and cuttings are an irrevocable part of the landscape, but there are other, smaller items which have survived almost unnoticed for 140 years. A number of the original narrow bridges beneath the line now form major traffic hazards. An original bridge of fine proportions and carried out in cast iron still spans the Rochdale Canal just north of Middleton. The railway line was reconstructed at a later date on a new bridge to the west, but the old bridge remains. Some of the over-bridges here, too, are the originals.

The old Rochdale station was demolished some ten years ago, and even its splendid replacement has been replaced—by a modern structure more in line with current passenger demands but, thankfully, carried out in the characteristic yellow brick of its predecessor. But north of Rochdale, where the real trans-Pennine section begins, it is stone all the way. The over-bridges are stone, the cuttings are lined with stone, and although the stone-flag fencing which once bordered the line has gone, Gauxholme Bridge retains its castellated parapet and Hebden Bridge station has been—mercifully—renovated to its 1880s splendour. (That, of course, is Lancashire & Yorkshire, but fragments of the original stations remain also.) Part of the original Hunts Bank station is still there, and a tiny part of Todmorden station is probably a portion of the first station building; certainly it has the neo-classical look of the early Manchester & Leeds buildings and a canopy supported by cast iron columns close to the running track.

The railway line between Manchester, Todmorden and Sowerby Bridge remains a tribute to the skills of Stephenson, Gooch and the rest, but it is also a celebration of the craft of the navvy. These men built the line with little more than picks and shovels, muscles and guts. They lived rough in turf huts by the side of the line, they brawled and argued and they struck terror into the hearts of the local populace. In May 1846, a dispute over wages paid to the English and the Irish building the East Lancashire Railway through the Irwell valley led to a riot in which 2,000 men were involved. 'Many men on both sides,' it was

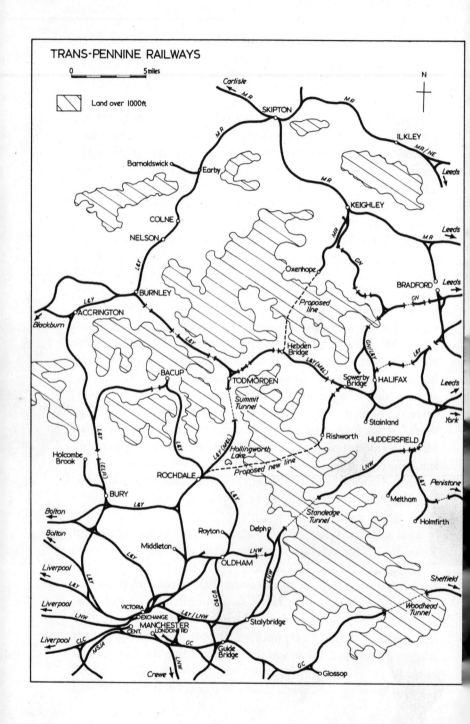

reported, 'were severely beaten and a number of the Irish were driven from their houses.' Two policemen were repeatedly beaten when they tried to intervene.

Of the local navvies, a contemporary report said:

The strongest and most distinguished . . . are collected principally from the hills in Lancashire and Yorkshire and are men of the finest physical stamina in the country. In strength and energy they have not been exceeded by any in the United Kingdom and equalled by none on the continent. . . . On average they are stated not to last beyond their fortieth year; but with fair treatment they would last in health and vigour until their term of three score.

It is not at all surprising that when Malcolm Macdonald chose to write a novel around the building of a railway he should choose the construction of the Summit tunnel of the Manchester & Leeds!

11
'THIS IS NOT
A LOVABLE LAND'

The coming of any railway anywhere was bound to have a considerable effect, but the building of the Manchester & Leeds, the first trans-Pennine line, was a traumatic experience. By the time it was finally opened, railways existed on both sides of the Pennines and the gap between the Oldham Road and Liverpool Road stations in Manchester was the only break in a continuous line from Liverpool to Hull. The early timetables show connecting services from Manchester and Leeds to Sheffield, Birmingham, Leicester, London, York and Darlington, Preston, Lancaster and Newcastle. And the railway up the Roch valley, through the Summit tunnel and down Calderdale was immediately a vital link between the systems to west and east.

The actual physical impact of the railway on the countryside was irrevocable. Forty years before, the canal had come, but that had stepped gently up and down, in a line sympathetic to the valleys it ran through. The railway, of necessity, charged its way through the Pennines, almost literally chewing up anything that was in its path.

Admittedly, in the narrowest and most 'difficult' part of Calderdale the railway clings to the side of the hill, dipping in and out of tunnels, but its viaduct at Todmorden (nine arches lifting the line well over 50ft above the valley) dominates the town centre totally. In the Walsden valley the line is very apparent, only a few yards away from road and canal, crushed between the rising hills. Indeed nowhere throughout its length is it more than a quarter of a mile from the canal that preceded it.

The Impact of the Railway

The village of Summit felt the full impact of the coming of the railway. Wherever there was an outlet from one of the working-shafts for the tunnel the debris was simply dumped in high mounds. One of these appears by the side of Owler Clough waterfall on the county boundary and provides a handy look-out point for the impressive views along the Summit Pass towards Todmorden; another stands isolated and rough as when it was dumped, in the middle of the village. Massive amounts of stone were quarried locally for the engineering works on the railway and the quarry sites remain, scarring the landscape over the tunnel 'top' between Summit and Calderbrook. Hundreds of trees were cut down or simply covered up during the building and Summit lost those woods that had survived the building of the canal.

A mile or so south of Summit, the building of the railway obliterated Ealees manor house at Littleborough and the arches of the viaduct over the Halifax road shadowed the Dissenters' chapel. A mere fifty years before, the northern end of the Roch valley had been a wooded Pennine clough, disturbed only by the 'meandering river'. Now it was a major traffic artery, carrying two main roads, the canal and the railway, both of them the first—and busiest—routes across the Pennines. At Rock Nook, close by the tunnel entrance, the Todmorden turnpike, railway and canal came close together—so close that it was possible to throw a stone clear across them. Even the river no longer meandered; it was confined to a cast iron channel carrying it across the railway. One has only to stand at this point today to see the total change brought in so short a time. Along the road stand small weavers' cottages, pressing close against the rock face to the west. On the opposite side of the canal stands Rock Nook Mill, which is built into the 'Backing Hole' of the early canal scheme and is, again, pressing against the sheer rock face. Ahead is the tunnel mouth itself and alongside the tunnel mouth is Sladen Wood Mill, built on a piece of level land created from spoil taken from the tunnel workings. Here, the river is totally underground.

Jessie Fothergill

Clearly, the old ways had gone. This was the 'industrial society'. Within a few years a local novelist would write (of a fictitious village, but one immediately recognisable as Littleborough):

A Town Village, the place is ugly, it is dirty, it has tall chimneys which vomit forth smoke, that clothe land with a garment of smuts. It has mills and factories swarming with dingy looking Hands, whose garments, as they pass by distribute odours of oil, fustian and cotton fluff. It has a long black canal, the banks of which are fringed with factories, stone-quarries and foundries . . .

Generally, keen winds blow, and often smutty rain comes sweeping athwart the smoke from dawn till dark . . . but the canal at last finds its way into green fields . . . and nearby are hedges which perhaps in late summer, have been known to be guilty of—not bursting, for vegetation here never bursts, but of slowly, tardily and reluctantly unfolding into a semblance of hawthorn bloom. Such trees as there are are stunted and scrubby . . . the hills are long bleak moors, naked and gaunt for three quarters of the year, and for the other quarter, dressed in a bright garment of purple heather, yellow bracken and scarlet bilberry leaves . . . This is not a lovable land, its very aspect suggests hardness, chills, bleak winds, howling and whistling over the desolate moors.

This was written by Miss Jessie Fothergill, a remarkably good but long out-of-print mid-Victorian novelist, who was living at Sladen Wood House, just behind the mill, at the time. Her father had taken over the mill from King & Co (hence its local nickname 'King's Shed'). He was later to go into partnership with Alexander Harvey, to form Fothergill & Harvey, one of the 'definitive' names of the textile industry.

The Machine Breakers

Hand-loom weaving, once the mainstay of the area, had sunk to a low ebb. Some weavers still hung on, desperately poor and in an altogether wretched state. As early as 1826 it was reported that cotton weaving had 'got to starvation work'. This observation of conditions comes from Haslingden, but was typical of the problems all over the area:

I don't think anyone could make over 9s a week, work as hard as they could. Food was dear—salt 4d a pound, broken sugar 8d, lump sugar 1s. But working people didn't use much sugar. They had porridge and milk. I have had porridge twenty-one times a week . . . all the farmers had loom shops and fancied the power looms was going to starve them to death.

That morning, we set off to the loom-breaking. When we had got

106

on the road we saw horse soldiers coming towards us. There was a stop then. The soldiers came forward, their drawn swords glittering in the air. The people opened out to let the soldiers get through. Some threw their pikes over the dike and some didn't. When the soldiers had come into the midst of the people, the officers called out 'Halt!' All expected that the soldiers were going to charge, but the officers made a speech to the mob and told them what the consequences would be if they persisted in what they were going to do. Some of the old fellows from the mob spoke. They said 'What are we to do? We're starving. Are we to starve to death?' The soldiers were fully equipped with haversacks, so they emptied their sandwiches among the crowd. Then the soldiers left and there was another meeting. Were the power looms to be broken or not? Yes, it was decided, they must be broken at all costs.

The results of this confrontation were not typical. Troops were brought in and demonstrators killed; conversely, the owners of the dreaded power looms were also murdered and, inevitably, retribution followed. Occasionally, though, disturbances were ended more covertly. Magistrates swore in a large number of 'special constables' who went in the dead of night and arrested local ringleaders. The following morning, it is reported in one case:

The inhabitants were all in amazement, one telling another that such and such had been fetched from his bed . . . The method of arresting them and taking them away at once so completely put a stop to the breaking of power-looms . . . The rioters were so frightened that a-many durst not go to bed in their own houses. Some left the country; others hid themselves for weeks, some in one place, some in another, some in coal pits—some, who few, if any would have thought would have been guilty of such a crime.

In September 1841, Mr Sharman Crawford, MP for Rochdale, told the Commons that 136 people in the town were living on 6d a week, 200 on 10d, 500 on 1s, 850 on 1/6d and 1,500 on 1/10d. Five-sixths of these people had hardly any blankets and 85 had none. There were 46 families with no coverings at all.

Conditions in the less populous areas were admittedly a little better. The inhabitants of the smaller settlements in the Pennine valleys could get out on to the moor and trap the occasional hare or collect berries or dock-leaves (for the locally prized and still available Dock Pudding). Riots there were, and loombreakings, and the Luddites met in secret on many a moor-top. The military presence was there, too, but the local people knew the moors and the soldiers did not. They could scour the valley sides for days without knowing that the men they sought were lying just a few feet away, observing their every move. The machine-breakers had friends (and eyes and ears) everywhere, safe houses and an instinctive 'feel' for the countryside. The militia had none of these and they were wholeheartedly detested by the local populace. Many of the soldiers, too, were sympathetic to the locals (as shown in the account of the Haslingden confrontation). Among the 'long bleak moors, naked and gaunt for three quarters of the year' they had little success. The loom-wreckers went about their work; the owners of the mills went about armed and guarded and fearful; the rioters assembled.

The Women

The word 'mob' tends to suggest a male assembly, but the women often played a prominent part in the riots. After all, they were the ones who had to make ends meet on the pitifully small amount of money available to them. Often the women were in the front of the mob, screaming abuse at the military, and daring the soldiers to fire on them. Often they were successful in preventing a riot turning into a massacre; occasionally, they were not.

Strangely, it was ultimately the womenfolk who 'broke' the turbulence. Factories could well use female labour. Women, conscious of the desperation in the home and attracted by the money offered in the new mills, sank their pride (or rather, that of their husbands) and took employment. Women, strong of character thereabouts, became the backbone of the burgeoning textile industry.

If anyone is in any doubt as to the strength of these women, the following extract from the memoirs of a hand-loom weaver who lived on the moors between Bacup and Todmorden may clarify the position. She recalled a time when, as she said, 'There was plenty of Law, but a sad lack of justice dealt out to the workers'. The account is all the more powerful since it was written down in the dialect form:

Yei, it wur hard wark for poor folk i 'thoose days. We geet sixpence a cut for weyvin' and in a whool week, working long hours, we couldna get through moore nor about nine or ten cuts—for they were twenty yards long apiece. That would mak five shillin' a week at most; and when we had finished 'em we had to carry 'em on our backs two or three miles to th'takker in. I can remember my owd man once takkin his cuts in and he tramped through th'weet and th'snow on a cowd winter's mornin' and when he had getten his cuts passed by th'Takker In, he axed him if he would gie him a penny to buy a penny moufin to eat as he wur goin back whoam. But th'Takker In said to him, 'Eh, Mon! If I wur to gie thee a penny it would be giein thee 'th' profit 'ut our maisters get fro' a cut! [At the time the masters were probably getting a clear guinea from each cut.] Noa, it'll never do to gie thee pennies i' that reckless way, Jone.' It wur hard wark i'thooas days, I con tell thi, to get porritch and skim milk twice a day, wi' happen a bit o' bacon on Sundays. Once I had to go fro' near to Stoodley Pike across Langfield Moor wi' mi cuts. It wur a rare cowd mornin', verry early, before it were gradely leet. I when I get theer, th'Takker In—eh, an' they wur hard 'uns wur thoose Takkers In, whooa says, 'Hillo! Are yo here sosoon, Betty? Warn't yo' fley'd o' meetin' th'Deil this mornin' as yo' come across Langfield Moor?' I says, 'Nowt o'th'sooart. I wur nooan feart o' meetin' th'Deil up on'th'moor, for I knew hangments weel that I'd find th'Deil when I geet here!'

Walking that old track today, as one can, it is easy to sense the old woman trudging along in the half-light of the early morning, probably, if she admitted it, fearful of the devil, aware of that strange Pennine 'something' just behind her shoulder. Perhaps she sang to keep up her spirits. A stout Wesleyan hymn would be fitting, but she may have chosen the openly defiant words of a verse written by Joseph Hodgson, a hand-loom weaver from Blackburn:

> Ye weavers of Blackburn, come hear to my song
> When I sing of tyrants I seldom do wrong;
> For if they transport me to Canada's wild shore,
>
> Then I shall have freedom when I have sailed o'er;
> Free from slavery,
> Fetters and knavery,
> Never tormented with tyrants again.

It is not surprising that the weavers of Lancashire, with mem-

109

ories of their own tribulations at this time, should have sided so firmly with the Northern States during the American Civil War. That war plunged them into another desperately depressed period, but they persisted, insisting that they knew all too well what slavery meant.

The old days and old ways had gone indeed, and the new world of the factory and the all-embracing textile industry engulfed the people of Lancashire and Yorkshire. The hand-craftsman's world fell apart, a traumatic experience matched only by the cataclysmic collapse of the cotton industry in the last fifteen years. Present-day balladeers (like Fivepenny Piece, born and bred within sight of the Pennine Hills) have chronicled the latest trauma, but, able as they are, their songs have not the defiant, clog-shod clout of Joseph Hodgson!

12
THE L & Y

Contrary to what might have been expected, trade on the Rochdale Canal continued to expand after the railway opened. By the middle 1840s, canal operators in the North of England were falling over each other, endeavouring to lease their canal to a railway company or amalgamate with them. It was not until 1855 that the Rochdale entered into an agreement with the Lancashire & Yorkshire Railway and other companies. The arrangement was for twenty-one years, but was continued until 1888.

In 1888, canal traffic reached a peak of nearly 700,000, equivalent to fifty boats a day. Many of the mills received their coal by canal and a great quantity of timber was carried. Most of the manufactured cotton goods leaving Todmorden left by barge. And canal transport was not as slow as one has been led to believe. Thirty or forty tons of cloth could leave Todmorden about six in the evening and be delivered to the wharf of a Manchester warehouse early the following morning.

Up to 1887, the Rochdale Canal Company acted as toll-takers only, but in that year they started acting as carriers in their own right. Clearly, this was a more efficient way of handling the canal's business and in 1891 they used 2,018 boats fewer to carry roughly the same tonnage as was carried in 1887. Most of the barges were horse-drawn with a three-man crew, and although sometimes it was a family crew with living accommodation aboard, the drivers also worked in stages of about ten miles—a relief driver and fresh horses being available at the end of each stage. The barges were capable of carrying up to 80 tons each and had curiously feminine floral names (*Poppy, Bluebell and Tulip*). The shorter Calder and Hebble boats had much more powerful names (*Energy* and *Enterprise*). Between them, the floral and the powerful made the Rochdale Canal by far the most successful of the trans-Pennine canals and one of the most successful in the country.

In the early days of the Manchester & Leeds Railway, the canal had a brief moment of glorious superiority. Until the opening of the Heywood branch, passengers for that town were carried there from Blue Pits station (now Castleton) by barge. Apart from this temporary service, there was no regular passenger traffic on the Rochdale Canal (unlike the Bridgewater where there had been a packet-boat service from Worsley to Manchester from an early date), but there were many pleasure trips, organised by local societies.

Branch Lines

The railway, too, was expanding. A branch to Oldham from the main line was surveyed by Stephenson and Gooch in 1840 and opened on 31 March 1842. The old Mills Hill station was closed and a new 'Oldham Junction', soon renamed 'Middleton' was built. (History coming full circle, fifteen years after the demolition of Middleton Junction Station, Greater Manchester Transport was proposing the construction of a new station to serve Middleton and Chadderton, to be named Mills Hill!)

A new line down to Victoria station was built and a connection with the Liverpool & Manchester finally made, but not without considerable difficulty. The Duke of Bridgewater (a familiar protagonist from the past) wanted a southern connecting route, much on the line of Stephenson's proposals of 1830. Eventually, the Liverpool & Manchester agreed to the connection, but not until after the Manchester & Leeds had indulged in a little gentle blackmail by commissioning a survey for its own line to Liverpool. The new station at Hunts Bank was opened on 1 January 1844 and, with Her Majesty's permission, named Victoria.

The Huddersfield Line

On the Yorkshire side of the Pennines, further branches were surveyed. One, from Cooper Bridge along the Colne valley to Huddersfield, was presented to Parliament in 1844, but withdrawn when the Huddersfield & Manchester Railway and Canal Company's Bill was introduced. The construction of this second trans-Pennine line was authorised on 21 July 1845. This alternative line was significantly shorter than the Manchester & Leeds and became part of the London & North Western Railway in later years. Ultimately, it was the route used by the trans-Pennine Inter-City expresses from Liverpool to Leeds and York and the earlier line via Todmorden was down-graded. Importantly, the Act which authorised the building of the Manchester–Huddersfield line incorporated the Huddersfield Narrow Canal and at the same time Sir John Ramsden's (the Huddersfield Broad) Canal, which linked Huddersfield with the Calder and Hebble, was also purchased.

The route from Manchester went via Stalybridge and up the Tame valley to a tunnel parallel to the old canal tunnel under Standedge, and in fact connections were made between the two tunnels. Then it ran down the Colne valley to Huddersfield, then via Dewsbury and Batley, through the long Morley tunnel and on to Leeds. Huddersfield had a long and complicated battle to get the railway to come, but when it came, the town celebrated with a Corinthian-columned station which is magnificent not just by Yorkshire standards but by national ones!

The existence of plans for a branch from the railway between Leeds, Dewsbury and Manchester to Bradford resulted in a Bill to promote a branch from the Manchester & Leeds at Mirfield through Heckmondwike, Liversedge and Cleckheaton (the *When We Are Married* heartland!) to Bradford; but it was thrown out.

However, a third branch, this time on the Lancashire side, was successful. It was to be from the main line at Miles Platting to Ashton, Stalybridge, and there was to be a further branch to Ardwick to terminate 'in the same field' as a branch of the Sheffield, Ashton & Manchester Railway. Eventually, the Manchester–Sheffield line provided the third Lancashire–Yorkshire link in the form of the formidable Woodhead route with its own summit tunnel constructed at phenomenal cost in both money and life. This was in being by 1845.

Other railways were being built at this time, notably those connecting the two halves of Lancashire separated by the Rossendale spurs of the Pennines. The line connecting Bury and Haslingden was originally conceived as a canal, but was built as a railway, part of the East Lancashire Railway which eventually linked the cotton towns between Burnley and Blackburn to Manchester. Thomas Gooch was concerned here, too, and he was

113

faced with a dilemma when he was asked to survey a branch from Heywood to Bury for the Manchester & Leeds. Eventually, the directors of both companies agreed and urged him to survey the line, and it was extended from Heywood to Bury.

The Lancashire & Yorkshire

By 1847, the Manchester & Leeds Railway directors felt that the title no longer accurately represented their lines. It was planning to amalgamate with the Wakefield, Pontefract & Goole, which would push its operations practically to the east coast. The company had also planned a branch from Todmorden up the Cliviger Gorge to Burnley and was proposing a new route into Leeds. A Parliamentary Bill was introduced and on 7 July 1847, the Manchester & Leeds became the Lancashire & Yorkshire Railway. In the words of the Directors:

> The extended district now embraced by the lines belonging to the Company has suggested the propriety of adopting a title more expressive of the extent and importance of the united system than that of the parent company, and your Directors suggest that the future title of the Company be the Lancashire and Yorkshire Railway.

The Lancashire & Yorkshire title remained appropriate right up to the time of its amalgamation with the London & North Western in 1921; apart from its joint ownership of the Axholme Railway in Lincolnshire and of a short portion of line at Stalybridge (which was wholly incorporated into Cheshire in 1894), the railway was entirely within the Roses Counties.

It was never one of the great railways of the world and was not even the largest provincial company. (That distinction went to the North Eastern Railway.) It had none of the glamour of the London & North Western, with its slogan 'The Premier Line', or the cushioned splendour of the Midland, and it certainly never inspired the loyalty bordering on adulation afforded to the Great Western. Its image was very much that of the North of England at the time—hard working, intensively developed, a little grimy, innovative yet allowing itself few indulgences and above all commerically clear-headed to the point of boredom!

114

It amalgamated—for instance with the East Lancashire Railway and the various lines in the Sheffield, Barnsley, Huddersfield and Goole areas in 1859 and the West Lancashire Railway in 1897—and it expanded, pushing branch lines determinedly up the Pennine valleys. It both reached out to the coasts and filled the land in between with an intensive network of railway lines. At its greatest extent, the Lancashire & Yorkshire reached from Hellifield in the north to the South Yorkshire Coalfield, and from Fleetwood and Liverpool to Goole. In truth it reached much further than that; its ships served Drogheda and Belfast across the Irish Sea and a galaxy of European ports—Copenhagen, Hamburg, Delfzjil, Amsterdam, Rotterdam, Bruges, Ghent, Zeebrugge and Dunkirk from Goole.

It had short branches from its Huddersfield–Penistone line up to Meltham and Holmfirth and one from North Dean, Halifax, through very difficult country to West Vale and Stainland. In collaboration with the Great Northern Railway it built a curious line from Holmfield (between Halifax and Queensbury) to St Paul's which was a second Halifax station 713ft up on the western edge of the town.

A New Main Line

The railway line up the Ryburn valley was not originally intended as a branch line at all, but as a 'cut off' for the circuitous main line through Hebden Bridge and Todmorden. A line from Sowerby Bridge to Ripponden had been proposed as early as 1845, but had clearly been intended as a branch line; the later proposals planned a substantial double-track line leaving the main line at Sowerby Bridge, running up the Ryburn valley to Ripponden and Rishworth, then tunnelling under Blackstonedge to emerge on the Lancashire side near Hollingworth Lake.

Work on constructing the line began in 1873, but there were enormous difficulties and the line was not completed until August 1878 (and then only as far as Ripponden). At that time it was reported that 'It is expected that the Company will continue the line under Blackstonedge to Littleborough', but the railway had only reached a little further up the valley to Rishworth by 1881.

Interest was revived the following year when proposals were issued for an entirely new Leeds to Liverpool railway. The Lancashire & Yorkshire reaffirmed its intention to build the line under Blackstonedge and the new railway proposal was dropped. Presumably the L & Y really did intend to build. Sowerby Bridge station had been rebuilt in splendid style with platforms on both the old and new 'main lines' and the booking hall spanning the space between and the branch itself had been constructed to massive main line standards. In the event, nothing further developed and the line between Todmorden and Sowerby Bridge remained the only link between the western and eastern halves of the railway.

On the Lancashire side, the Railway built branches to Rochdale via Oldham and Milnrow and from Rochdale up the Whitworth valley to Bacup. This branch had the distinction of including the highest point reached on the Lancashire & Yorkshire. (It was very nearly 1,000ft up, at Britannia, between Shawforth and Bacup itself.) It also had one of the most elegant railway structures—the high, slim viaduct over Healey Dell, which fortunately still exists (although the line itself has gone) and is used as a footpath link in the Healey Dell Nature Trail.

Lancashire & Yorkshire railway engines faced some fearsome gradients: 1 in 27 on the branch from Middleton Junction to Oldham, 1 in 40 on the infamous Baxenden Bank between Haslingden and Accrington; and on the Bacup branch it was uphill all the way from Rochdale to Britannia (1 in 60, then 1 in 50 and finally 1 in 40—a full seven miles of it).

The Railway considered itself to be primarily a freight-mover (and the most common illustration of the Lancashire & Yorkshire in the railway books is a variation of the 'heavy coal train near Mytholmroyd') and it moved vast quantities of coal and iron in both directions over the Pennine link. Passengers came a poor second—very often a very poor second. Criticism (of bad timing, dirt and general discomfort) reached a peak in the late 1870s and in the 1880s the railway started to put its house in order. On the main line, for instance, stations were almost totally rebuilt; Rochdale was in fact resited altogether. Of these 1880s stations only Hebden Bridge remains in anything like its old style—an evocative gem and recently refurbished.

Photographs of the railway in Lancashire & Yorkshire days are remarkably rare. Here a Yorkshire-bound express passes Green Vale Mill, Littleborough, a few hundred yards south of Summit Tunnel. The locomotive appears to be one of the two batches of 4–4–0 designs built at Horwich in 1891 and 1894. By this date the original 'stone flag' fencing to the line had been replaced by standard timber fencing. The mill was the most southerly of the complex of Fothergill and Harvey's mills at Rock Nook

Summit, Littleborough, was an outpost not only of the Rochdale system but of the whole South Lancashire municipal network. From 1907, Todmorden ran buses from the town to Steanorbottom (on the county boundary) half a mile along the pass from Summit. Later, the service was extended to meet the trams at Summit. After amalgamation in 1974, West Yorkshire Metro PTE instituted the first regular services between Littleborough and Todmorden by extending their route down to Littleborough Square

With Blackstonedge and the Ealess valley in the background, a pleasure party prepares to leave Littleborough Wharf in 1910. These barge trips were popular and usually cruised along the long three-mile pound to Rochdale, through two locks and turned at Hartley Farm, Castleton, where refreshments were available. The barge is a standard 70ft × 14ft Rochdale Canal Company craft. Note the ice-cream tub in the bows

Scammonden Bridge is said to be the longest single-span arched bridge in Europe and crosses Deanhead Cutting, the deepest transport cutting in Europe. The fixed arch has a span of 410ft and carries the A6025 Elland–Denshaw road, here running along the ridge to the east of the Ryburn valley. Constructing the 180ft deep cutting involved removing 4 million cubic yards of rock. A special blasting technique was developed to produce rock fragments of the correct size for the embankment for Scammonden Dam without further sorting or treatment

At this time, a new station was built at Smithy Bridge, between Littleborough and Rochdale, using stone excavated during the construction of the Ripponden branch and primarily placed there for the benefit of travellers to Hollingworth Lake. It was fractionally nearer to the lake than was Littleborough itself and gaudy posters appeared all over the L & Y system extolling the beauties of the Pennine resort. The station survived until the early 1960s, when, along with Newton Heath, Middleton Junction, Walsden, Eastwood and Luddendenfoot (not to mention the branch lines) it was closed and demolished. Curiously, this was just about the time that the area round Hollingworth Lake began to develop. Within ten years a sizeable community of, mainly, commuting families developed—without the advantage of commuting by rail from their local station!

The Lancashire & Yorkshire had no monopoly on trans-Pennine transport nor did it own all the interesting branch lines. The legendary Delph Flyers were the property of the LNWR, the Midland had a line running roughly parallel to the Leeds and Liverpool Canal from Colne to its main line at Skipton and the Great Northern ran a massively engineered line across from Queensbury by way of Denholme and Cullingworth to Keighley. Then there was the Worth valley line which pushed up from Keighley to Haworth and Oxenhope. At one time there were plans to extend this line by way of a tunnel under the hills to join the Lancashire & Yorkshire main line at Hebden Bridge. The plans never materialised and the branch line was left to run, to close, to be revitalised and to emerge as *The* Worth Valley Railway. It is far, far busier now than it ever was and the station and yards at Haworth are as popular an attraction as the parsonage on the hill above.

Improvements on the Lancashire & Yorkshire included the introduction of slip-coaches. A section of a trans-Pennine express could be detached and, under the control of the guard, come to a halt at an intermediate station. A number of trains from Yorkshire slipped a portion at Rochdale, which portion was taken on to Southport by the shorter line from there via Bolton. In the reverse direction, a 'Burnley' section was slipped as the train approached Todmorden. This technique lasted for a long time—well into the London, Midland & Scottish era.

119

Victoria Station

The Railway had a complexity of services out from Manchester. Trains ran to Bacup via Bury or by way of Middleton Junction, Heywood and Bury, or Bacup could be reached by way of Rochdale and the branch up the Whitworth valley. Oldham had trains direct or via Middleton Junction, Burnley services via Accrington or Todmorden. Gradually, the Lancashire & Yorkshire extended and improved its terminus at Victoria. In 1844, when it was first built, it had a single platform and the elegant neoclassical building on Hunts Bank. By the time it was completely extended in 1909 it had seventeen platforms, seven of them 'through' roads and the others for local trains to Bury, Oldham and so on. The Bury branch was electrified at the outbreak of World War I and at the time there were plans to extend electrification over the suburban routes.

The final station is a tribute to a 'substantial' railway, and the equal of any station in the country. The facade of the concourse building is impressive, garlanded with an elaborate canopy emblazoned with exotic (and somewhat incongruous) destinations. 'Rotterdam' rubs shoulders with 'Goole' and 'Bury'. Inside it had a small buffet in impeccable Art Nouveau style, a sombre memorial to the employees killed in World War I and a glorious map of the L & Y system painted on clear white tile. And of course the whole complex was linked to the LNWR's Exchange station by the famous Platform 11, the longest, they said, in the world.

Much of the roof over the 'through' platforms went in the ferocious Manchester blitz and Exchange station went during the inevitable cuts. The line through Manchester's 'Metroland' to Bury survived (just), but the short and convenient line linking Rochdale to Bury, Bolton and beyond disappeared, as did the services to Middleton, Royton, Rawtenstall, Bacup and Holcombe Brook. Even Haslingden and Accrington were left without their direct link and Colne and Burnley only served via Blackburn.

In 1978, British Rail announced its intention of demolishing the old office block opposite the main Victoria station concourse and giving the station buildings a face-lift. After a short, abortive fight, the office block went, to reveal the full splendour of the station's facade for the first time since it was built. The facade was cleaned, the buffet renovated with most of its features intact and the whole project handled with a sympathy that surprised many of the local conservationists and enthusiasts. The splendid map, far from being obliterated, was not only cleaned and re-painted, but the all-important Lancashire & Yorkshire network was picked out in red, the original black reserved for other (ie minor!) lines.

By the time the railways were 'grouped' in 1923, the Lancashire & Yorkshire and the London & North Western had already amalgamated, and on grouping, the L & Y became part of the London, Midland & Scottish Railway. The locomotives survived for a long time—well into the British Railways era—although most of the L & Y carriages, having creaked their way through World War II, disappeared shortly afterwards. Then some faceless, nameless official high up in British Railways decided that it was not in keeping with the spirit of a nationalised railway undertaking to have a main line that ran east and west and decreed that the old Manchester & Leeds main line should be designated Midland region to Hebden Bridge and Eastern Region from there to Leeds. The Roses Counties were to be severed for good and all!

The Decline

The trans-Pennine Inter-City expresses arrived, running by way of the Standedge and Huddersfield route to Leeds and the old Lancashire & Yorkshire main line was down-graded. At times its future was in doubt. The rolling stock deteriorated and the stations looked like disaster areas. Local government reorganisation meant that money could come in to subsidise some services; on the Yorkshire side the West Yorkshire County Council subsidised the old main line as far as Todmorden and on the western side Greater Manchester Transport put money in to save the Manchester–Oldham–Rochdale services. Travellers on both sides of the Pennines were encouraged to use their railway, with some heartening results.

In 1979 indeed, British Rail even improved the service.

121

Additional trains were introduced at peak hours and the GMT/BR service from Manchester via Oldham to Rochdale was extended back to Manchester by the direct line.

Even after this, the middle section of the line was left in a curious position. From Rochdale to Todmorden the line is controlled not from Manchester or Leeds, but from Preston. The smart publicity material issued by West Yorkshire PTE exhorts passengers from Todmorden to use its Calderdale line but not the services to Manchester. The spectacular and potentially useful route up the Cliviger Gorge is heavily used for freight but carries only the intermittent enthusiasts' special.

But at least the line remains—a lasting tribute to the navvies, the engineers and that oddly evocative Lancashire & Yorkshire Railway. Mile for mile, it is one of the most spectacular rail trips in the country, plunging through tunnel after tunnel, clattering across viaduct after viaduct with the ghosts of those 2–4–2 tanks chuffing away up into the enfolding hills! Many things have happened in the years since the Manchester & Leeds was built. Slip-coaches have come and gone, steam has come and gone, services and tracks have gone, probably for ever. But there are still eight tunnels between Littleborough and Sowerby Bridge, and if you carry on to Leeds there are thirteen. Nothing can alter that.

13
REFORMERS AND TRADERS

The Hungry Forties produced a revival of Chartism and Chartists were among the rioters who caused havoc during the 'Plug Riots' of 1842. Now the working classes were not alone; they had sympathisers in some places that would have seemed surprising ten years before. Alexander Harvey, for instance, the father of Gordon Harvey and a founder of Fothergill & Harvey, the textile firm, was active among the poor of Manchester at this time. Horrified by what he saw in the slums of the time, he became converted to the Free Trade doctrine and the new radicalism. He joined the Anti-Corn-Law League and gained the friendship of its organiser, Cobden, and the Bright brothers.

During the appalling time which preceded the repeal of the Corn Laws he worked unceasingly for the relief of the starving and it is said that in later years he could never recall those times without weeping. Noting that mill-hands and carters were too exhausted after the week's work to attend church or enjoy the Sabbath he initiated a Saturday half-holiday which was, by 1843, taken up by most of his fellow merchants in Manchester.

Fielden and the Ten Hour Act

In Todmorden, the Fieldens also tried to alleviate the distress among their workpeople. Up to 1836, matters relating to the poor had been dealt with by a 'vestry' consisting of householders, 'ley' or rate payers, clergy, churchwardens and sidesmen, but with the Poor Law Act of that year a Board of Guardians was elected for each township. In the well-named Hungry Forties they faced tremendous problems and the Fieldens assisted by employing their men—some 2,000 of them—in reclaiming land and repairing roads, paying them half their normal factory wages. The enterprising Fieldens, one-time Quakers and latterly upholders of the Unitarian faith, had by this time made a town of Todmorden. 'Honest John' Fielden was MP for Oldham when, in 1847, he was largely responsible for the passing of the

Ten Hour Act which regulated the hours to be worked by factory labour. A Blackburn worker, writing in 1849, the year after the Act came into force, commented:

> It is only now that operatives can enjoy gardens and other advantages they have gained by the Act. Formerly they could not take a walk in the mill yard, but were locked inside the mill from 5 in the morning until 9 at night. For 38 years of my life I was so closely immured in the factory that I never saw a field of corn cut by the hand of the husbandman. I had no opportunity of witnessing such a sight except on Sunday and that was the day the harvestman rested from his labour.

Cobden and Bright and Free Trade

Chartists and Reformers ran on parallel courses throughout the troubled years. Anti-Corn Law League supporters started with two tremendous advantages: they had brilliant, dedicated leaders like Richard Cobden and John Bright of Rochdale, eminently respectable Establishment figures; and they had money enough to back their lengthy campaign. By 1843, the League had bombarded the public with some 9 million tracts and among them was a substantial booklet sent to every voter. It urged them:

> You are an Elector. To you is entrusted the privilege of choosing the law-makers. It is a trust for the good of others; . . . Think solemnly and carefully, before you decide.

The gist of the message was set out plainly:

> . . . you will be entitled to choose between a bread taxer (one who withholds corn from the people) and a candidate who will untax the poor man's loaf.

And, to reinforce the importance of the decision, the voter was reminded:

> Remember, above all, that your decision will be recorded on high, and that you will be called on to account for your vote at that dread tribunal when all mankind will be judged—not by their professions, not by their prayers, but when the blessed will be told 'I was hungered and ye gave me meat'.

124

The League did not confine itself to exhortation and suggested retribution in the hereafter. It acted in strictly practical ways, principally by buying land to provide freeholds (and hence voters for the League's supporters). The Anti-Corn Law League provided a small but articulate pressure group within Parliament, and once Robert Peel was converted (helped, no doubt by the potato famine in Ireland) the Repeal Bill was passed, on 26 July 1846.

The Anti-Corn Law League and the Free Trade movement overtook the Chartists and by the time the Repeal Bill was before Parliament the *Manchester Guardian* was able to report that the room used by the militant Chartists of Mossley in the Tame valley 'is now closed, and the boards where the orators held forth and made known the principles of the *Northern Star* are converted to a resting place for swine'.

The Chartists had set out their Six Points (universal suffrage, vote by ballot, equal electoral districts, abolition of property qualifications for MPs, payment of MPs and annual Parliaments) and some had been achieved. It was, at least, a beginning. Oddly enough (in the light of more recent troubles) it had two 'wings'—physical and moral. Probably it never seriously threatened the stability of the nation, but looking back in 1868, one Joseph Livesey was to comment:

> Comparing the last twenty years with the previous thirty years, I don't hesitate to say that free trade has saved this country from revolution, and has been the forerunner of that contentment, tranquillity and progress which have marked this latter period.

The Rochdale Pioneers

In this period, too, came the idea of co-operative trading which was to become a major influence. Although it has been suggested that the navvies working on the railway at Littleborough may have formed a co-op of sorts, the first practical manifestation of the ideal came in Rochdale when the Pioneers opened their shop on 21 December 1844.

Their entire stock consisted of 28lb of butter, 56lb of sugar, 6cwt of flour, a sack of oatmeal and some tallow candles—all of which had been bought for £6.11s.11d. For the first three months, the store was open on Saturday and Monday evenings only, but soon the Society found that it had to open every evening except Tuesday; additionally, it was soon able to pay its first 'divi' of 3d in the pound. By the end of the year the membership had trebled and the 'Co-op' had made a trading profit of £21.

Pure, rather than cheap food was the aim of the Rochdale Pioneers. Many products of the time were adulterated (a Liverpool firm actually patented a machine to press chicory into the shape of coffee beans) and, partly in order to ensure purity, the Rochdale Pioneers soon bought their own corn mill. The Pioneers' idea spread rapidly and soon there were Co-ops all over the area. Todmorden and Bacup were among the early converts and even lowly Littleborough had its own 'Store'. Ultimately, it had many, consisting of a central nucleus (Provision, Ladies' and Gents' Outfitting, Footwear, Furnishings, Greengrocery, Fishmonger and even Clogger and Abattoir) housed in separate shops and splendid, domed premises in the main shopping street, and the all-important branch shops scattered around the edges of the small town.

By 1851, the Co-operative Movement had 130 Societies and more than 15,000 members, and the setting up of the North of England Co-operative Wholesale Society in 1863 brought the Societies together into a powerful union. 'Th' Store' became a way of life for countless people and 'Wheatsheaf' (the Co-op's brand name) literally a household name.

Some of the larger Co-ops were far more than merely shops. Both Rochdale and Todmorden had libraries and reading rooms; the librarian at Rochdale would lend out 200 books a day. The acquisition of knowledge—often knowledge for its own sake—was becoming an important factor in the everyday life of the working man of the area. Literary and scientific societies, debating societies, groups devoted to botany, science and engineering flourished, and Professor Sedgwick, a geologist who visited Manchester in 1842, commented that he had met, 'operatives whose brows were smeared with dirt and whose hands were black with soot . . . who in many ways were my superiors'. And in *Mary Barton*, published in 1848, the novelist Mrs Gaskell wrote:

In the neighbourhood of Oldham there are weavers, who throw the shuttle with unceasing sound, though Newton's *Principia* lie open on the loom to be snatched at in working hours but revelled over in meal times or at night. Mathematical problems are received with interest and studied with absorbing attention by many a broad-spoken, common-looking factory hand. It is perhaps less astonishing that the more popularly interesting branches of natural history have their warm and devoted followers among this class. There are Botanists among them, equally familiar with either the Linnaean or the Natural system, who know the name and habitat of every plant within a day's journey of their dwellings; who steal the holiday of a day or two when any particular plant should be in flower, and tying up their simple food in their pocket handkerchiefs, set off with single purpose to fetch home the humble-looking weed. There are entomologists who may be seen with a rude-looking net, ready to catch any winged insect or a kind of dredge with which they rake the green and slimy pools; practical, shrewd, hard-working men who pore over every new specimen with real scientific delight.

Writers and Poets

The Pennines had a half-dozen or so 'native' writers, often writing in their own dialect. Again, they were practical, shrewd, hard-working men, but men with the gift of words to be used to explain and decorate their lives and their surroundings. Samuel Laycock, for instance, originally from Marsden in the Colne valley but resident in Stalybridge and who wrote 'Welcome Bonny Brid' at the time of the cotton famine during the American Civil War. It is said that if a Northerner knows two dialect poems, one will be 'Welcome Bonny Brid'. The anti-American poems that Laycock wrote at the same time are forgotten, but the words of 'Welcome Bonny Brid' (and for that matter, the sentiments) live on. For all its straightforward sentimentality and its regular, traditional rhythm, the undertones of despair, anger and frustration are there. A father, deep in the poverty brought by the Lancashire weavers' resolute refusal to handle American cotton, cradles his new-born son in his arms and explains in his own everyday tones the problems of the world they both face. There are too many children, times are bad and so on. The final lines:

127

But though we've childer, two or three
We'll mak' a bit o' room for thee.
Tha'rt prettiest Brid we have i'th'nest
So 'utch up, closer, to mi breast.
Ah'm thi Dad.

are often taken merely as a sentimental rounding-off for what has
been a fairly harrowing tale, but one suspects the 'Ah'm thi Dad'
may be a sudden, horrifying realisation of the man's position.

There was John Stafford Clegg (himself a weaver) and the
doyen of them all, Edwin Waugh of Rochdale. His works, unlike
many of the time, are still read and there is a flourishing society
dedicated to propagating his works and writing in the local
patois.

The chapels, and to a lesser extent the Anglican Church, contributed to the passion for learning. All over the area men and
women assembled to listen, to learn and to interpret. The first
public lecture organised by the Manchester Mechanics' Institute proved the point. 1,400 people managed to gain admittance
to the lecture and as many again were unable to get in to the Institute.

Emigration

For some, though, emigration was the answer to the problems
besetting the area. George Smithers left Old Sowerby and
settled in Pennsylvania in the early 1840s. In two of the surviving
letters he wrote to his uncle, Titus Spencer of Quickstavers,
Sowerby, he talks of his new life as a farmer and relays messages
from and information about other men from the Sowerby
district also settled in the USA.

> I saw John Hanson this Spring and they are doing well. They have a
> lease on a farm of a hundred acres for ten years. The farm belongs
> Benjamin Sykes, and Sykes is keeping tavern in Philadelphia and is a
> verry intemperate man . . . Mary Hallowell who married John
> Bailey wishes me to write to you concerning the money that was left
> by her Grandmother Walker . . . the family is scattered and there is
> none but Mary and William living in Philadelphia . . . Old Eli Hallo-
> well is living about ten miles from here in New Jersey. He is combing
> wool, but he leads a verry intemperate life . . .

We hear that there has been a great famine in Ireland and a great deal of money sent from this country to assist them, but the Irish that is emigrating here by the thousand say that there has been no famine there and that they never heard of it until they come to this country. Now you live so near you certainly know whether the people is starving to death there or not and I wish you to inform me the true state of the matter. I will conclude my letter by sending our respect to all our connections and all inquiring friends . . .

At the end of the second letter he adds, almost casually;

The people of the United States have got the Gold Fever and a great many of them have left to go to Calaforna to dig gold. I suppose it is a verry rich place and under no control from government and it is a verry dissipated place.

Back home in the old country, things were at last looking up. Trade expanded and contracted, encouraging and alarming the expanding towns, but soon there was a distinct change in emphasis and attitude. The combination—of Reform, learning, growing expertise, the Co-operative Movement and the particular egalitarianism of the North, philanthropy and business sense—was the fuel that fired the powerhouse.

14
'AND WAS JERUSALEM?'

The Pennine towns had a number of benefactors. Their generosity may not have been entirely motiveless, but their achievements were considerable. The Bolton district had a number of model employers who ran village communities alongside their mills and Jacob Bright of Rochdale, the Whiteheads of Rawtenstall, the Fieldens of Todmorden and the Grants of Ramsbottom (in spite of their involvement in the Truck system) were acknowledged as enlightened mill-owners, light years removed from the stern mill masters of legend.

Titus Salt left the North the most consummate expression of the benefactors' philosophy. Born at Morley of determined Nonconformist parents in 1803, by 1850 he owned six mills in Bradford, had made a fortune, was acknowledged as a progressive in local politics and was on the point of retiring. Instead he built Saltaire. He bought land conveniently sited on the line of the canal and railway near Shipley and commissioned the Bradford architects Lockwood and Mawson to build not only a new mill but a whole town.

The first building was, not unnaturally, the mill, at the time the largest in the world and designed to the very latest standards. On the roof was a tank containing 70,000 gallons of river water as a fire precaution and beneath the building was a rain-water storage reservoir of 500,000 gallons capacity, the water being used for processes within the mill. All the shafting which drove the machinery was housed below floor level, obviating some of the appalling accidents that were frequent when an operative got entangled in the belt-drives. There were cranes and other devices designed for operation with the minimum of human force and a form of air-conditioning was installed. Warm or cold air could be circulated throughout the working areas and the foul air drawn up the 250ft chimney.

The town contained 850 houses of various sizes, but each with kitchen, living room, three bedrooms, yard, privy and refuse pit. A good water supply was installed and disinfectant was issued during the not infrequent outbreaks of cholera. Public baths, a school, an infirmary and almshouses for the sick and elderly were built. In 1871 the Saltaire Club and Institute was opened. It provided a reading room, library, science laboratory, art room, classrooms, billiard room, armoury and gymnasium. In the same year, Saltaire Park was opened. The crowning glory, as in so many towns, was the church. In this case it is a Congregational church, but Salt also donated money to Methodists and Baptists.

Gordon Harvey

By Titus Salt's standards, the achievements of Gordon Harvey of Littleborough were modest. Rather than creating a new community he left an indelible impression on an existing one. By the standards set by Cobden and Fielden his career as an MP was fairly undistinguished, but his ideas were a good half-century ahead of their time and even his moderately progressive attitudes were not adopted in the establishments of his fellow mill-owners for many years.

Alexander Gordon Cummins Harvey was born in Manchester in 1858 into a family steeped in the radicalism of the Manchester school. At fifteen, Gordon Harvey was already writing essays on land reform and was an ardent political debater. At sixteen he entered Owens College (now Manchester University) to study mathematics, although secretly he dreamed of being a barrister or entering politics.

Harvey Senior was a partner in Fothergill & Harvey and a mill at Summit, taken over in 1859, had been enlarged and run mainly by his partners, Harvey himself devoting his time to the Manchester end of the business. His old partner (Mr Fothergill, the father of author Jessie) died, a second withdrew and Gordon Harvey was forced to leave university and, after a period acquainting himself with the complexities of the textile trade at firms in Oldham and Wigan, took over the running of Sladen Wood Mill shortly after his twenty-first birthday.

The weaving shed at Sladen Wood was described as 'neither the best nor the worst of its kind', but a description of it gives one a graphic picture of the working conditions at the time and is in

131

sharp contrast to the new factory at Saltaire which was already twenty-five years old:

> Very little provision was made in winter time for the heating of the sheds, or in summer for cooling them. Nothing was done in regard to ventilation. A few outlets at the top of the sheds supplied fresh air, but even these were stopped up by the weavers when they got the chance. Many times in winter the temperature was at freezing point, and when 'steaming' began to be introduced to make the warps weave better, the condensed moisture dropped all over the place. In summer time 'degging' or watering cans were employed to moisten the floor of the shed and keep the temperature humid.
>
> Provision for the comfort of the workpeople was meagre. Many of them came from a distance bringing their meals with them, and the only way to warm them was to take them to the boiler house and place them on the boiler; and at meal times the weavers could either eat their food in the boiler house among the coal dust, or stop in the cold weaving shed. The only provision for drying the clothes of the operatives was again the boiler house—if you got the chance. Otherwise the wet clothes had to be put on again at night when you went home. No special cloak rooms were provided so the clothes had to be hung on pegs in the damp weaving shed . . . the place was lit with gas, and when it had to be kept burning—as happened many times during the winter months—for whole days together the carbon dioxide nearly knocked you down when you came in from the outside air.

The 1880s were prosperous years for the cotton trade and in 1886 Fothergill & Harvey built Rock Nook Mill on the opposite side of the canal where they began to spin their own yarns. Significantly, they also began to build houses for the workers and in the same year Gordon's younger brother, Ernst, joined him at Littleborough. Ernst Harvey had a gift for mechanics and he was soon able to take over the entire direction of machinery and processing, leaving Gordon free to devote more of his time to local and ultimately national politics.

Liberal—but Radical

Politically, Harvey insisted he was not simply a Liberal, but 'a Radical who is willing to act on Liberal lines'. He first stood as a Parliamentary candidate in the election of 1900 and his speech to the Liberal council in Rochdale sets out with devastating clarity the doctrines he held for the whole of his political life. In the address he said:

> I am in favour of the widest possible franchise and one vote apiece
> . . . I believe in complete religious equality, and consider the con-
> nection between Church and State harmful to both . . . I believe in
> the extension of local self-government, and that feeling goes with me
> throughout . . . I want a large measure of land reform. My ideal is
> the nationalization of land. I think the municipalization of it is within
> the range of practical politics, and that there ought to be a measure
> passed whereby a real and fair share of taxation shall fall upon the
> landed interest.

This was relentlessly radical stuff and Rochdale lapped it up. For fifty-nine of its sixty-eight year history, the Rochdale con-stituency had returned a Liberal member, and those members had been leaders in political thought. ('I would rather sit for Rochdale,' Richard Cobden had written to John Bright, 'than for any other place in England; for Rochdale Liberalism has heart enough in it to back up a man against the autocratic section of the Legislature.')

Referring to the House of Lords, Harvey observed:

> Oh, Gentlemen! We are a slow and easy-going lot of people. The
> champion of the people's rights 250 years ago declared that this
> House was useless, dangerous and ought to be abolished. That is my
> ideal; but I am content as a practical man to accept what I believe was
> the solution suggested by Mr Bright that, if necessary, we should for
> the present content ourselves with the restriction of their Lordships'
> veto . . .

The Boer War was at its height and Fothergill & Harvey were benefitting from the orders placed by the government. All the same, Harvey, peaceful man though he was, went for the mili-tarists with all his guns blazing!:

> I am against the policy of grab and bully. I detest those methods
> which lead to war . . . I am not one of those people who compare the
> Empire to a prize ox and judge it by its size. There should be no fal-
> tering, no temporizing with this great bombastic military doctrine
> that is growing up round us.

The opposing Conservative candidate was the sitting member, Colonel Royds, and he appealed to the electorate to support a 'patriotic' candidate, and Tory posters showed the Boers praying for the return of a Liberal government. Gordon Harvey was also spending time supporting the Liberal candidate for the adjoining Middleton constituency, which in those days was a vast area reaching from Middleton itself to Todmorden, taking in Littleborough, Milnrow, Whitworth and several other small mill towns. At the election a Socialist candidate polled 900 votes and Harvey lost by nineteen votes.

In 1906 it was a different story. The contest was described as one of the fiercest ever fought; in spite of a 2,500 vote for a Socialist candidate, Harvey had a 1,500 majority over his Conservative opponent, the sitting member. Even accepting the fact that 1906 was the year of the Liberal landslide, it was no mean achievement.

The Powerhouse

It was these Edwardian years that saw 'the North' at its most identifiable—rich, opulent, influential and, importantly, articulate. It spoke with a clear, strong progressive voice. It would have no truck with fools or idlers. It was not only the industrial heartland of the country; it controlled a trading empire that conquered the world. The textile industry, particularly cotton, reached its zenith and the North was supreme in mechanical engineering. The industrial empires were mostly still within the control of one family living in splendid mansions, but still with their feet planted firmly between the looms or lathes.

National Education

Harvey was firmly in favour of the severance of Church and State and an advocate of National Education. As a result of the 1870 Education Act, School Boards had been formed and Todmorden had had a Board School by 1874, with, predictably, a Fielden (Mrs Samuel) as an enthusiastic member of its board. Littleborough held out against National Education and Gordon Harvey had a tremendous fight to get a Board School established

Nutclough Mill, Hebden Bridge

Hebble Hole Bridge, Colden Water, Hebden Bridge (on the Calderdale Way)

Hebden Dale and Heptonstall: the Long Causeway can be seen curving away into the distance

locally. Littleborough had Church of England, Nonconformist and Catholic schools, but Harvey insisted that it ought to have one of the new National Schools. 'Because our parents used rowing boats,' he observed, 'must we never have steamers?'

His 'disestablishment' stance could not have helped his cause, but in the end Littleborough made its application for a new school. It was the last application in the country. Even then, amendments to the original Act very nearly destroyed the whole plan, but surreptitious adjustments to the plan got it accepted and Harvey laid the corner-stone in 1901. Even by present-day standards it is a clean, elegant and workmanlike design and has needed little improvement since it was built.

'Anti-disestablishmentarianism' reached a peak in 1906 and Mrs Beswick Royds of Pike House (a descendant of the Colonel who had been a signatory to the original canal proposals of 1766), a loyal churchwoman, offered to pay for anyone who would go to London to demonstrate against the proposals to sever Church and State. Not unnaturally, many people accepted, including the whole Littleborough Brass Band!

Muck and Brass

The North was, in those days, decidedly plain, blunt and honest. Its wealth was often demonstrated, as it was in its town halls. Halifax Town Hall was built between 1859 and 1862, and designed by no less a person than Sir Charles Barry, architect of the Houses of Parliament. The style is officially 'North Italian Cinquecento' but has been more accurately described as a Victorian extravaganza. The mason who carved ornament for both the Houses of Parliament and Buckingham Palace was employed to decorate the Halifax building and the whole fantastic edifice is topped by a strangely attractive ziggurat-like spire. Halifax also has the Wainhouse Tower, originally built in the 1870s as a dye-works chimney, but remaining as a public monument and as extravagant a Victorian Folly as any anywhere.

Rochdale Town Hall was conceived as a copy of a Flemish cloth hall, and another notable architect, Crossland, designed it. No expense was spared and the interior is alternately sombre (with heavily carved stone and deep-toned stained glass) and glittering with gold, green and pale blue. The Great Hall is just what its name implies—huge, hammer-beamed and dominated by a superb (and recently restored) organ console. The entrance hall beneath is known as the Exchange, and the original hope was that it would be used as a cotton exchange.

Manchester, of course, topped the lot with its monumental Waterhouse building, which trumpeted the success of Cottonopolis. Leeds characteristically chose a more restrained, but none the less opulent, neo-classical style. Even Todmorden, with a population of only about 18,000, has a magnificent town hall, designed, significantly, by John Gibson, who was the architect of Dobroyd Castle.

Legend has it that Todmorden Town Hall stands astride the old border between Lancashire and Yorkshire (and for that matter the Saxon kingdoms of Mercia and Northumbria). The windows on the 'Yorkshire' side are decorated with a fleece and those on the 'Lancashire' with a cotton plant. The building stands suitably close to the roads, hemmed in by the surrounding buildings. The architect may have fancied it remote, at the end of a long avenue, like the classical mausoleum it evokes, but placed as it is, in the very centre of the small, bustling town, it symbolises the sympathies and practical achievements of the era. Todmorden may now be simply a part of the Metropolitan Borough of Calderdale, but its town hall speaks of a proud and independent past!

The symbols of the great golden age are all around in the towns pushing up into the Pennines. There are few Victorian 'halls' but many mansions. Most are solidly traditional (and a few are monstrous), but here and there are examples of houses evoking an earlier period. (The extensions at Townhouse, Littleborough, carried out for the Harveys in the early 1900s, are more in keeping with the old house across the way than with the Georgian 'new' house.)

Edgar Wood

The North had its own native architects, notable among them Edgar Wood. Wood was born at Middleton in 1860, the son of a prosperous mill-owner. His work was much influenced by

138

William Morris and the Arts and Crafts movement and later on by the advanced designs of Charles Rennie Mackintosh. Incorporated in many of his designs is a sympathy for the local style, which married well with the principles expounded by Morris.

He built the Long Street Methodist chapel in Middleton, a number of houses nearby and two pubs in Rochdale, the 'George and Dragon' close by the M62 bridge at Castleton and the 'Victoria' on Spotland Road. Both are evocations of the naturalistic, domestic-scale style popular at the time. Later, Wood went into partnership with James Henry Sellers, who was born in Oldham and whose father had been a mill-worker. Together, they designed some remarkably advanced buildings. Two schools in Middleton (Durnford Street and Elm Street) illustrate a style that was clean, clear, almost ascetic, relying heavily on proportion and almost devoid of unnecessary ornament. Yorkshire, though, had two of Edgar Wood's most outstanding designs. Banney Royd, Edgerton (Huddersfield) was the largest house he built. Outside it carried through the traditions of the Yorkshire manor house, but inside was his own version of a modern style; his clock tower at Lindley, near Huddersfield, is said to be the most complete 'Art Nouveau' structure of his career. But again, it is Art Nouveau with a definite Yorkshire accent!

The later designs are startlingly modern. A group of shops in the centre of Middleton was built in reinforced concrete in 1908, with flat roofs and panels of decidedly jazzy zig-zag ornament running down the facade. A house built in 1910 for the Editor of the *Middleton Guardian* is, again, flat-roofed. The materials are traditional red brick, but the proportions are entirely modern. Both Wood and Sellers were more than just architects. Both designed furniture and decoration for their houses as well as individual pieces. Their work was sophisticated, yet comfortably scaled and totally unpretentious. Typically, both were renowned on the Continent and almost totally ignored in Britain. The first definitive exhibition of their work was not held until 1975 when, to coincide with European Architectural Heritage Year, the clear significance of their work was outlined at the Manchester City Art Gallery.

Wood and Sellers were outstanding, but they had their followers, particularly locally. Many of the smaller Pennine towns

139

have terraces of small houses echoing the feel of the farmsteads on the moors. At Deanhead, Littleborough, for instance, are two splendid rows of houses on the main road to Todmorden, their windows mullioned in the fashion of the weavers' cottages, the door hinges with a hint of the Art Nouveau about them. At Timbercliffe, also, is a group of comfortable houses which blend into the landscape. Perched high above the Fothergill & Harvey mills, they were built by Gordon Harvey in a strictly non-traditional material. On the opposite side of the canal to Sladen Wood Mill there had been a pipe-making works, utilising clay mined on the hillside above. Harvey installed a plant to make use of this and various waste materials which, formed into 'concrete' blocks, were used to build the houses. Even this was not the first use of an unorthodox material locally. A group of houses alongside the canal just above Littleborough Lower Lock was built in concrete block by E. Taylor & Co, a local firm who later built the splendid Edwardian Victoria station. The terrace, called, appropriately, Taylor Terrace, was built in 1870 and was a pioneer example of this form of building.

The early years of the twentieth century also saw the ultimate development of the cotton mill. Huge glass and red-brick 'industrial palaces' rose five, six or more storeys into the murky gloom. Each had its massive engine hall ('room' is a totally inadequate word to describe the structure enclosing the massive engine that drove the factory) and each had its tall chimney, often emblazoned with the name of the mill in stark white tiles. And the names were remarkable—'Eagle', 'Clover', 'State' and, in Todmorden, a massive 'Mons'. There were thousands upon thousands of looms, millions of spindles. (After all, Lancashire was clothing the world in cotton and Yorkshire was warming it in worsted and wool.) Illuminated at night, and backed by the blackness of the hills, they looked, as someone said, like so many ocean liners. It was an appropriate description—these were, we should remember, the grandiloquent days of the *Mauretania*, the *Olympic*. And the *Titanic*.

140

15
CORPORATION
AND INDEPENDENT

Trams never quite conquered the Pennines, but came near to doing so. A long route up the Colne valley from Huddersfield reached Marsden, only about seven miles from the Waterhead terminus of Oldham tramways and about the same distance from Haddens, the end of the line that ran up the Tame valley from Stalybridge. Indeed, at one time there was a plan to take a line from Springhead, Oldham to Saddleworth, with a terminus less than five miles from Marsden. Huddersfield, incidentally, operated Britain's first 'municipal' tramway system, starting in 1883.

Halifax trams ran to Sowerby Bridge and on up the Ryburn valley (as far as Triangle) and to Jumble Hole Clough on the boundary between Hebden Bridge and Todmorden. The Halifax tramway system had the distinction of being the hilliest in the country. Some routes climbed to well over 1,000ft above sea-level from the town centre 700ft below. It is said that scarcely 100yd was actually on the level and even the depot was on a definite slope!

On the Lancashire side, steam trams started running from Rochdale to Littleborough in the 1880s as part of the ponderously-named Manchester, Bury, Rochdale & Oldham Tramways Company Ltd (which, in any case, never got to Manchester). In the Oldham area the line was standard gauge (4ft 8½in) but the trams in Rochdale were the narrow (3ft 6in) gauge. The undertaking was municipalised in 1904, and electrified and extended. The line from Whitworth was extended up the valley and over to Bacup (parallel to the railway line and also touching 1,000ft at Britannia) and the Littleborough route was extended to Summit in August 1905.

Summit was the outpost of the vast tramway network that covered South Lancashire, all on the same standard gauge. In theory it was possible to run a tram from Summit all the way to the Pierhead at Liverpool, to Altrincham or to Hazel Grove on the far side of Stockport.

141

The Todmorden Buses

Todmorden, half way between Summit and Hebden Bridge, clearly had a problem. If it chose to bridge the gap, which gauge should it choose? Todmorden did, in fact, apply for permission to build nine miles of tramway, which would have almost closed the gap and taken trams up Cliviger Gorge as far as Portsmouth, but the application was dropped in favour of buses. They started running on 1 January 1907 and were only the second municipal motor bus undertaking in the country (the first had been at Eastbourne). Todmorden had actually taken delivery of its buses late in December 1906 but shrewdly chose not to license them until the New Year.

Todmorden's buses were legendary. Within a few months of the start of operations one ran off the road and into a shop-window. Commended for his bravery in staying at the wheel, the driver (with typical Todmorden honesty) commented, 'I only stayed there because I was too frightened to jump!' On the Portsmouth route there was a low railway bridge which required careful negotiation. The crew would make sure that everyone on the open top deck was sitting down and then the bus would plough its way through. In later years, Leyland developed the 'side-gangway-low-roof' bus for Todmorden Corporation in order to cope with this bridge. A loose grate in the road provided the driver with a signal. If he heard a 'clank' as his wheels passed over it he knew he was in the middle of the road and could safely pass through the bridge. An extension to the town's bus garage was built to fit these buses, but when, in later years, the awkward bridge was rebuilt and then standard height buses were introduced it was found that the new buses would not fit into the garage!

A route was established over the moors to Bacup and, not surprisingly, the bus engines heated up to a frightening degree. Drivers kept a pocketful of spare gaskets which they fitted when necessary, heavy leather gloves being provided for the purpose. The early buses show distinct signs of their tram ancestry, with a curved parapet to the front of the top deck, but in later years many adaptations were made—and some complete bodies built—by a local joiner.

Pirates

The Summit route met the Rochdale trams at the terminus a mile and a half up the valley from Littleborough, as the Todmorden service did not run through to Littleborough itself. Indeed, for a while it terminated at the Todmorden boundary at Steanorbottom and passengers were faced with a hefty walk to the trams over the hill. Eventually, the legalities were unravelled and the Todmorden buses turned at Summit. Not until a 'pirate' service began to operate from Burnley to Manchester did the Todmorden buses begin to run through to Rochdale. The Claremont Company started a service from Burnley down the Cliviger Gorge to Todmorden, then via Summit and Rochdale to Manchester. It was found to be technically illegal since the company was plying for hire within Todmorden, where the municipal buses had a monopoly, and legal action ensued. The bus operator cleverly arranged with shopkeepers in Cornholme, Todmorden and Walsden to check the number of people waiting there and telephone the 'orders' to him in Burnley. This meant that legally he was 'booking seats' on a private-hire coach.

This prompted the Todmorden Omnibus Company to institute a through service to Rochdale on Saturdays and for many years these were the only buses which genuinely bridged the gap. It was not until after 1974, when local government reorganisation brought about the West Yorkshire Metro PTE, that the bus services from Halifax and Burnley to Todmorden were extended from Summit to Littleborough on a regular daily basis.

The 'pirate' bus service naturally affected the railway too as the railway services from Burnley to Todmorden and from Todmorden to Littleborough and Rochdale ran right alongside the road but were less convenient for passengers. So the railway and Todmorden Corporation joined forces to operate the Todmorden Joint Omnibus Company and (until the days of West Yorkshire Metro) the dark green Todmorden buses carried the crests of both undertakings—first the LMS and then British Rail.

Todmorden also ran a bus service to Hebden Bridge, then over the moors to Oxenhope and Keighley. At Bacup their buses met the trams coming up the valley and over the hill from Rochdale and the trams running along the Rossendale valley towards

Rawtenstall and Haslingden. Through-running of the trams was not possible here as the Rossendale trams were 4ft gauge, as were the other tramways on the northern side of the Rossendale Fells. Between Rawtenstall and Bacup is Waterfoot and from here trams ran up the side valley to Lumb and Water, terminating only about 4 miles from the Burnley trams over the moor.

Trolley Buses

In the Irwell valley between Bury, which had standard-gauge trams, and Rawtenstall is Ramsbottom, and this was the site for an early trolley bus system running from Holcombe Brook down to Ramsbottom and across the valley to Edenfield. Ramsbottom UDC had originally intended to run trams, and the depot was prominently labelled 'Ramsbottom Tramways', but pioneer trolley buses were brought in instead. They ran from 1913 until 1931, when they were replaced by buses.

Trolley buses were not common in the Pennine area. Keighley, like Ramsbottom, had an early system which was abandoned, Huddersfield converted from trams to trolley buses (running them up the Colne valley to the same terminus at Marsden) and, on the Lancashire side, Ashton-under-Lyne ran trolley buses. Bradford, on the other hand, went in for trolley buses in a big way and it was not until the 1970s that their smart, pale blue buses disappeared from the steep hills of the city. One of the last routes to be abandoned ran to Shipley, only a few miles from Keighley, which had operated trolley buses from Ingrow to Oxenhope, Keighley to Oakworth and Utley to Sutton between 1913 and 1921. Bradford, in fact, shared the distinction with Leeds of operating the first trolley bus route in Britain—Laisterdyke to Dudley Hill. For a short time, Halifax ran a trolley bus service on an experimental basis from King Cross to Wainstalls, both high on the western slopes of the town. The service only operated for five years from 1921.

Corporation Transport

Most of the tramways in the area were abandoned by the early 1930s (although a few, notably in Bury, Blackburn and Bradford, lingered on until after World War II), and the great days of the municipal bus operators began. Each town had its own distinctive colour scheme and often ran joint services with adjoining authorities. Lancashire had the largest network of these municipal undertakings in the country and the streets of every town were alive with colour.

In Rochdale, for instance, one could see the red and cream of the Manchester Corporation buses (running the joint service from Rochdale to Manchester via Castleton and Middleton), the green of Bury who operated two routes between Rochdale and Bury, the deep plum red and white of Oldham together with the dark blue, red and white of Ashton who ran services between the three towns in conjunction with Rochdale itself. Rochdale, Oldham and Manchester Corporations combined on the 'express' route between Rochdale, Chadderton and Manchester. The occasional dark green Todmorden bus could be seen on Saturdays, and always the dark red Ribble and lighter red Hebble buses. In addition, for a short time in the 1940s, a private coach company, Yelloway, ran the express service to Manchester with an odd mixture of vehicles. For a while, indeed, they ran an old London bus of uncertain antiquity— sufficient to say it had an outside staircase! The 'native' Rochdale buses were a smart blue and cream and were deliberately kept free of advertising. The Hebble company operated one of a number of routes which finally spanned the Pennines. They operated from Leeds to Halifax and on over Blackstonedge to Rochdale; the West Yorkshire company was also much in evidence on the trans-Pennine roads.

Inter-running was not as common on the eastern slopes, but the colour was there, too. Huddersfield used a red and cream scheme, Bradford was blue and Halifax painted its buses (with uncharacteristic gaiety) green, orange and cream. What Yorkshire may have lacked in network operations, however, it made up for in titles. There was a Yorkshire Traction Company and the Yorkshire Woollen District Company. The latter ran routes round the small towns south of Leeds and Bradford and was aptly named.

The first great amalgamation came with the decision to pool the undertakings around Manchester under the name 'Selnec', an uncomfortable title made up from the initial letters of 'South East Lancashire/North East Cheshire Conurbation' and the forerunner of Greater Manchester Transport. This was to operate services throughout the new Metropolitan County and chose a brilliant (some said vulgar) orange and cream colour scheme.

When the West Yorkshire Metropolitan County was formed on the eastern slopes, West Yorkshire Metro buses made their appearance in mid-green and near-white. Both undertakings naturally had symbols to identify their buses and property, GMT a large 'M' and West Yorkshire a clever (some said contrived) circular motif made up of repeated 'W's and 'Y's. West Yorkshire, probably under pressure from the independently minded town lobbies, allowed the name of the new Metropolitan Borough to appear also and the buses in the area based on Halifax are Metro Calderdale while those running from Huddersfield are Metro Kirklees. West Yorkshire Metro Calderdale also took over the Hebble company, so now the multi-coloured authorities are reduced to two over most of the Pennine area, with just the occasional white ex-Ribble National 'stranger'.

Coach Operators

From the early days coach travel was popular and took a lot of the traffic away from the railways in post-war years. Every small town had (and indeed often still has) its coach operator and they often inspired great loyalty among the local inhabitants. Parties (who had previously gone by rail or even canal barge) took enthusiastically to the idea of the coach trip, as far back as the days of the open motor-charabanc. The sea-side towns (Blackpool, Morecambe, Bridlington and so on) were naturally the popular destinations, with many a sightseeing excursion through the Yorkshire Dales or circular of the Northern abbeys thrown in for good measure.

These excursions very soon established themselves as an intensive sub-network of routes covering the North of England on a regular basis. For many years, in fact, the private Yelloway Company operated a year-round service from Rochdale and the surrounding towns to London.

146

Legends (and horror stories) about the trams and buses abound and have been perpetuated, handed down through the years. Halifax's narrow-gauge trams, swaying up and down the steep hills, seem to have made a habit of turning over (particularly on the long, curving hill down into Sowerby Bridge). Rochdale's standard-gauge equivalents did the same thing on the curve at the bottom of the steep John Street descent to the town centre. More than one early wireless enthusiast, straining to pick up 2ZY Manchester on his earphones, fervently wished the tram bucking its way down the grade from Summit to Littleborough would bounce straight off the tracks and into the field! Todmorden and Ramsbottom ran small friendly operations, but even some of the bigger bus operators had their moments of relaxation. One Rochdale conductor could do a near-perfect imitation of a cat which had been trodden on, and many a lady stepping from the high platform of those rear-entrance buses has heard an alarming squeal! In earlier days small children were taken to see—at the appropriate time—a Rochdale tram-driver who sported an enormous white beard. They were told (and naturally believed) that it was Santa Claus.

Few reminders of the tramways now exist, even inside the museums. In 1972 the then Littleborough UDC demolished the last remaining example of the larger type of tram-shelter which had survived the bus takeover forty years before and very recently the last of the lamp-posts which at one time supported the overhead wires have been replaced. There is, however, one fragment of tramway history remaining in Rochdale. In fact it was rediscovered—a short section of track was uncovered when the local council was constructing a new roundabout. The track and the setts around it were incorporated into a parking bay alongside the new section of road. It stands—symbolically—at the top of the steep John Street hill.

Even today, legends spring up. There is the story of the West Yorkshire bus that went on an unexpected safari into alien territory. In June 1978, a derailment blocked the railway line between Hebden Bridge and Todmorden and commuters were being ferried past the blockage to a temporary railhead at Littleborough. Unfortunately, the Manchester controller for British Rail failed to supply a vital early morning train at Littleborough to take the passengers on to Manchester. So the driver was persuaded to carry on down to the city. It is said that a passenger directed him as the green and off-white bus thrust its way into the alien orange and cream heart of GMT. The run ended in the shadow of the old Manchester & Leeds building at Victoria station—no doubt to the relief of all concerned. They had used the route best known to the passenger who was directing and according to another traveller they crossed the canal many times, crossed the pioneer railway more than once and, he suggested, managed a bit of designated footpath as well! 'Trouble is,' he added, 'we left him on his own at Victoria. I wonder if he ever got back?' With stories like this being handed down, even the smart, sophisticated Passenger Transport Executives suddenly show a human face!

16
CO-OPERATORS
AND IDEALISTS

The Co-operative Wholesale Society celebrated its Golden Jubilee in 1913, the last full year of peace. The Committee reported at the quarterly meeting held at the CWS Headquarters at Balloon Street, Manchester, that sales for the first half of the year were nearly £15 million, 7¾% up on the same period in 1912. Over 3,000 delegates attended the General Meeting in Manchester on 20 September and, it was reported, 'heartily adopted' a resolution which stated:

> That this meeting, whilst rejoicing over the great progress of co-operation during the last fifty years, and the many benefits consequently accruing to the working classes, heartily congratulates the Co-operative Wholesale Society on the attainment of its Jubilee and desires to record its warm appreciation of the particular services it has rendered to the movement during that period. It also urges on all co-operative societies the necessity of increasing their support of the federation, so that the manifold advantages of co-operation, both distributive and productive, may be still further extended.

Special grants were agreed by the meeting—£4,500 to the various co-operative convalescent funds and £1,000 to Ruskin College, Oxford.

The co-operative movement had come a long way since the Rochdale Pioneers had bought a local corn mill. It had shirt factories at Manchester, Sheffield and Pelaw, at Desborough and Huthwaite. It wove its own cloth at Batley, wove blankets at Littleborough, tailored its suits and overcoats at Leeds, Manchester and Newcastle. It made jam at Middleton and biscuits at Crumpsall. Co-operation was more than a way of trading, more than a way of life even. It was an ideal that had grown from the tiny beginnings in Rochdale and been nurtured by socialism, the trade union movement, even by the egalitarianism fostered by the Nonconformist chapels and possibly even by the self-reliance inherent in its Northern roots.

Fifty years after the formation of the CWS it was immensely powerful and inspired unswerving loyalty. Two days after the Jubilee General Meeting in Manchester, the idealism and loyalty were put to the test and the power of the movement demonstrated.

The Irish Strike

A large-scale strike was taking place in Dublin and the British trade union movement had agreed to stand by its Irish colleagues. On Monday 22 September a deputation from the Parliamentary Committee of the TUC returned from Dublin and drafted a report on conditions among the workers there. The following afternoon the committee resolved on an immediate grant of £5,000 for the relief of the strikers. Next the committee approached the CWS in Manchester asking for their help. It was agreed that the Co-operative movement would be able to supply 30,000 food parcels, each consisting of 1lb tinned fish, 10lb potatoes, 2lb sugar, 12oz margarine, 4oz tea, and 2lb jam. Meanwhile, the sympathetic owners of the SS *Hare* had been contacted and they agreed to carry the parcels to Dublin. But they would have to sail on the Friday afternoon at the latest, if the parcels were to be distributed on the Saturday, in time for the weekend. That meant that the CWS had just forty-eight hours to assemble, pack and load the 30,000 parcels, plus another 30,000 packs of potatoes.

Potatoes were in stock and jam was held in quantity at Middleton; tinned fish was available from stock, but margarine had to be brought from Newcastle and tea from London; 27,000 CWS potato bags were brought by train from the depot at Goole. Some goods were even 'clawed back' from local retail shops. The movement had its own box-making plant at Longsight and this started supplying cartons to Balloon Street where the parcels were to be made up. The men at the CWS potato wharf at Oldham Road, Manchester worked from four in the morning of Wednesday, through the day, then the night and then the following day. The biggest labour of all was the packing. Scouts were sent out to scour the streets for the unemployed. The Manchester dockers were on strike and helped in the packing.

The Dining Room at Balloon Street had provided tea for 150 of the workers and gave supper and breakfast to 50. In the middle of the Thursday night the volunteers broke for a short time, found a pianist and, a contemporary report says, 'sang everything from Hymns to Ragtime songs'. At four in the morning there were sandwiches and tea and at 6.30am, 'A douche of cold water sufficed'. The report of this stage of the proceedings comments: 'Rich people with no occupation except to draw dividends, and bored even with that, might have found salvation here.'

Manchester docks were strikebound at the time, but the dockers broke their strike to load this special cargo and the *Hare* sailed for Dublin soon after 5pm on the Friday afternoon. The *Hare* reached Eastham, at the end of the canal, at 11pm, only to be trapped there by the fast-ebbing tide. Eventually, and alone, the ship made its way out of the lock and down the channel. A seaman aboard commented that he had 'seen her tied up on many a lighter night'.

The ship arrived in the Liffey at about noon on the Saturday. The writer of the report noted:

> A tug by the electric power station roused the harbour with a prolonged and joyous hooting. Then ship vied with ship, and the cheers of the crews overpowered the sound of ships' bells ringing. Cries of blessing and 'God Save Larkin!' came from the walls of the narrowing river and children ran to the point of the wall where the crowd stood in a dark line to receive us.

Other supplies had already been delivered to Dublin. The local Industrial Co-operative Society and the United Co-operative Baking Society in Belfast had supplied 12,000 loaves, and barrels of biscuits had been supplied by the CWS works at Crumpsall.

The reporter of this extraordinary episode is not slow to make his point:

> ... girls locked out from the local biscuit works, now ready to pack biscuits sent over as an additional aid ... When they heard of the CWS conditions, in comparison with their own, these smart young girls instantly would have entered CWS service, if it had been possible, leaving without hesitation their native Irish land and Dublin City ...

151

He even manages to work in something of a 'commercial':

> In houses where raspberry and apple bought round the corner had been thrown away as bad, the eager children found under the Middleton cover a little label inviting the return of the jam if unsatisfactory . . .
>   The gift was of the best, and as from their fellows. 'Ah now' said one (man) proudly (he had not eaten for twenty-four hours) 'it's themselves might be wanting our help some day.'

The report concludes on a thunderous note:

> For it was realised that it was not trade unionism alone, or co-operation alone; but for once a great common effort of the people. And of a great common effort the story will be told and re-told, amongst trade unionists and co-operators, this year and for many a year.

The next year, however, was 1914 and as surely as the Pennines are a physical watershed, the Great War was a watershed for the areas on either side of the Pennines. War memorials all over the country testify to the irreparable damage done by the war, but in the Pennine towns and villages, with their tightly woven relationships, the tragedies were that bit harder to bear. The ripples from each death spread out through immediate family, then relations, then friends and neighbours. Old people who remember those years say the sadness has still not quite left the smaller towns. One couple in Rochdale lost all six of their sons—five of them in one morning.

Harvey and the Great War

Gordon Harvey, who was wholly representative of the radical ideals of the immediate pre-war period and who entertained a vision of European unity and interdependence, was immeasurably saddened by the sight of the country dropping into war. On 6 August 1914 he wrote to his constituents in Rochdale, setting down his feelings clearly:

> We are at war and we must face the situation together. For the moment argument is out of place, and a statement of the views of any

individual as to the immediate causes would be heard, perhaps rightly, with little patience in the midst of the stupendous matters that confront us . . .

I have long held, and often asserted the view that, to avoid a European conflict, the only way was, not to arm the nations to the teeth, but to bring them closer together in a free and mutual understanding . . .

We have for the moment failed and those who believe in force and whose business it is to use force, are now in possession of the field. When their work is done I shall hope to lay once more before those who will listen to me the view of a common humanity, and it may perhaps turn out that the experiences through which we are about to pass will make them readier hearers.

I have spoken against foreign entanglements and at the proper time I shall claim that I have been justified by events.

I appeal to all my intimate political friends—men and women who still share my views—to stand with me in this attitude of patience for a time; for it is clear that for the moment we can do nothing. The war has not been of our country's seeking. We are in it and our first duty is to our own folk at home and in the field.

Not everyone agreed with Harvey. It was pointed out to him that his mills were, as they had been during the South African War, making money. His position was not an easy one. He was accused of being a pacifist and his detractors denounced him for having tried to resist the competition in armaments before the war.

In practical terms he set up a fund to send comforts from the factory to its employees serving in the forces and he was a contributor to the hospital for wounded soldiers near his home in Littleborough.

The League of Nations

Harvey's mind, however, was already on the post-war problem. In April 1915, the National Peace Council, of which he was chairman, issued a leaflet outlining his plan for preventing future wars. It advocated the setting up of a permanent Congress of Nations to sit as a court of arbitration on all international disputes. In a speech at Waterfoot, in the Rossendale valley, a year later, he refined this description to a League of Nations. He wrote:

153

The League of Nations—all Nations—jumps to one's heart and brain. We must have it. The telegraph, the 'phone, the flying machine, close association, internationalism—the sequence is plain. But the ground must be made smooth for the League of Nations idea. It will be a delicate plant, sown in the forest before being planted in the garden.

Harvey's health, and some say his spirit, was broken by the war and his ill health forced his retirement from Parliament before the election of 1918. On 22 November he wrote a few words of farewell and admonition to his constituents in Rochdale:

... Force has conquered force, and power has subdued power as was the only way in the situation in which the world was placed; and now a task infinitely more delicate remains to be accomplished; I mean that great change of heart and mind and soul all over Christendom which shall end war and league the nations in a common purpose...

Gordon Harvey's intensely human—and therefore fallible— approach to internationalism was outdated and the liberal/ radical idealism was swept away. The story of the co-operators' help to the striking workers of Ireland would not be 'told and retold'; the intervening years had seen the Easter Rising, Casement and the Bolshevik revolution. Many a Manchester and Bradford merchant had had a 'man' handling the Russian end of the business from St Petersburg; Manchester, in particular, had had its Baltic trade (and has a Danzig Street to prove it). It had had Engels as a resident and Karl Marx as a visitor, had applauded Charles Halle, had (and, for that matter, still has) a coffee shop, proprietors 'Meng and Ecker'.

The Clecklewyke Establishment

The trams had symbolised that earlier, settled and 'sure' life; probably Mrs Northrop took one home after the disastrous anniversary evening in *When We Are Married*. J.B. Priestley, looking back on his family memories, no doubt, structured the society accurately: affluent, certainly, but constantly reminded of its roots; a trifle pretentious, even slightly arrogant about its achievement. The women have their timeless gossip, the men their club (and one, at least, has a bit o' fluff on the side). The club is not the Athenaeum but the local mechanical or political and the extra-marital diversion is a brief fling with the flashy Lottie Grady rather than a permanent adultery.

They are Chapel, while the minister brought in to try to sort out the problem is 'Church'—and ineffectual. The young choir-master and organist has two things wrong with him: he is young and he is a Southerner, and therefore prone to rashness and, worse, la-di-da. We are told over and over that what is needed are words that are *serious*. But the words weaving their way through the situation are never serious. To find oneself (or think oneself) not legally married after twenty-five years of utter respectability is a subject for comedy. And that comedy comes from the North as much as from Priestley himself.

The comedy disappeared from view after 1918 and did not re-appear for fifty years. *When We Are Married*, performed by however incompetent a cast, on its home ground is more than the production of a comedy. Unconsciously, perhaps, actors draw on something in their minds, perhaps in their souls, which is there for all time. The world's first repertory company was established at the Gaiety Theatre in Manchester by Annie Horniman and it spawned many plays and playwrights. Then a later era threw up the writers of the working-class fifties and sixties. Much has been written about the North, and much more about the North for 'outside' consumption, but the stalwart *When We Are Married* goes soldiering on, the native audiences lapping it up and, in the process, tasting, one suspects, the bitter-sweet tang of remembrance. It was downhill after the Clecklewyke trams stopped running!

17
CHANGE AND DECAY

Regular through traffic on the Rochdale Canal ceased shortly after World War I (although the last complete navigation was not to take place until 1939 and some sections were in use up to 1945) and in 1923 the Canal Company sold off the supply reservoirs to Rochdale and Oldham Corporations. Industry had always used water from the canal for its processes, so the navigation channel remained intact and the sale to the corporations included provision for the continued supply of this water.

The canal had succumbed not (as many other canals) to rail competition, but to road transport. In the peak year of 1888 the canal had carried 686,000 tons, the equivalent of fifty boats a day; by 1921 this had dropped to 180,000 tons or about 12 boatloads a day, and in July of that year the Company ceased as public carriers and all the barges were sold off to a local firm of carriers. In 1906 and again in 1913 there had been exhaustive enquiries into the future of British canals and in each case the subsequent report had recommended the improvement of canals and their further exploitation, but in each case (and in many future cases) no action was taken.

The canal survived intact and chemicals were still delivered from Manchester to Littleborough by water right up to the middle 1940s. The Rochdale Canal was not included in the nationalisation plans after the war (largely because of its primary function as a water-supply to industry) and in 1952 the Company applied to close the section between Manchester (Dale Street) and Sowerby Bridge to navigation. The short length of canal linking the Ashton Canal to the Bridgewater was retained, ultimately restored and now forms part of the vitally important Cheshire Ring of canals.

Restoration Plans

Even though officially closed to navigation (which suggests almost total dereliction), most of the canal remained in its navigable state. Some of the narrow and inconveniently sited bridges were lowered and some short sections channelled; in addition the building of a new road put 300yd of canal underground at Sowerby Bridge and the M62 was constructed at virtual water level in the late 1960s. All the same, the substantial remains and the obvious leisure potential of the canal prompted the formation of a restoration society in 1974 and a report by Dr C.T.G. Boucher showed that restoration, although costly, was a practical aim. From its inception, the Rochdale Canal Society has had as its aim the eventual restoration to full navigable standards of the whole length of the canal from Manchester (where it meets the Bridgewater Canal) to Sowerby Bridge and the navigable Calder and Hebble Navigation. The Leeds and Liverpool Canal is still operational and a similar restoration body already exists for the Huddersfield Narrow Canal. The enthusiasts point out that, mile for mile, the Pennine canals have a greater potential than most other restoration projects: 1½ million people have the Rochdale and Huddersfield Narrow Canals on their doorstep and 7 million live within seventy miles of them. The growing tourist industry in the South Pennines suggests that the proposed Pennine 'rings' formed by the Rochdale, Huddersfield and Leeds and Liverpool Canals would be of great recreational value. Also, more recently, ecologists have drawn attention to their more commercial value.

The various sources of government aid available from 1976 have prompted a number of restoration projects at various places along the line of the Rochdale and volunteers have also carried out various renovations. County and Borough authorities have acknowledged, in varying degrees, the desirability of restoration and Rochdale, in particular, has been active. A short section of once-derelict canal was included in plans for a pioneer industrial improvement area and now presents a semblance of its appearance in pre-1914 days. Significantly, it is a practical (ie working) section with fully operational locks. Alongside the canal at this point are mills which remain a memorial to the traditional Lancashire trades. On one side is the factory of Petrie & McNaught, famous for the manufacture of the massive engines that drove the mills, and on the other bank are two massive structures in the developed style of the 'cotton palaces'.

Even in the 1920s, however, the textile industry was no longer totally dominant, though Lancashire and Yorkshire were to remain identified with it for many years to come. The traditional divisions still applied—Rochdale and Oldham were 'cotton', Halifax and Huddersfield were worsted and wool and the area in between mixed one with the other. Todmorden, for instance, though technically in Yorkshire, had a considerable section of its industry devoted to cotton, while Littleborough handled a large proportion of wool.

The 1930s naturally saw depression and the closure of some mills that were never to re-open as textile factories. Additionally, some new industry arrived. An 'artificial silk' (viscose rayon) plant was opened in Littleborough by the Dutch Breda Visada Company and nearby, the old Cloughfield Oil Works was taken over by another immigrant, Hess Products, later Armour Hess, and later still the multi-national Akzo-Chemie company. Industry diversified, but not, in the event, sufficiently to compensate for the decline in the traditional industries of the area.

The Traditional Calendar

The traditional 'calendar' nevertheless survived. New Year was as important as Christmas. (Some considered it more important.) Mummers paraded on New Year's Eve and were invited into the house to sweep out the old year and sweep in the new. These strange figures, humming monotonously and wielding their brooms, were disciplined to wordlessness, but as they were normally children, the householder could usually persuade them to break their vow by offering sweets! Easter brought the Pace Egg Play, a curious and ancient mixture of St George, Beelzebub and the warrior Bold Slasher. It existed in various forms all over the South Pennines and is still performed in the streets of Wardle village (near Rochdale) and at Midgley.

May Day was also celebrated, not as a labour holiday, but in the old fashion with maypole and dancers. Whitsuntide was the occasion for the church and chapel 'Walks'. Each place of worship had its huge decorated banner and this was ceremonially 'walked' round the district. The whole town turned out to see the spectacle. Often (but not invariably, since sectarianism

158

was still quite strong) all denominations would meet for a combined service and then disperse to their various rendezvous for an afternoon of sport and recreation at 'The Field', which was often one near the chapel or church. In some places the Walks were on the Whit Monday, but in others it was the Friday of Whit Week with the 'Trinity' weekend and Monday as a holiday.

The mills were still largely in the hands of the families which originally owned them and they retained their influential position in the community. The Littleborough Parish Church Whitsun procession would walk up to 'Honresfeld', the home of Sir Alfred Law, owner of Durn and Lydgate Mills and MP and church benefactor, before going off to its afternoon relaxation. By way of compensation, each child in the procession received a gift with the compliments of 'Sir Alfred'.

Throughout the year there were the church and chapel 'Anniversaries', massive occasions for special services and singing. This or Whitsun meant new clothes, and many a family would go into debt to provide the youngsters with new clothes for the occasion. The clothing club 'checks' were regular currency, giving many families access to easy and untroubling credit. A £5 'check' would mean 5/- down and then 5/- a week for twenty weeks, which was a 'finite' debt rather than the continuous credit of the present-day credit card. The big firms like Mutual & Provident took most of the business, but various local enterprises also existed. In Littleborough, for instance, the local Traders' Association organised its own scheme, with credit available only through its own members' shops. The system was financed by the interest paid by the check buyer and by a discount deducted by the shopkeeper which went to pay the overheads and the wages of a collector. In the grim Depression days it helped families and shopkeepers alike: the families could keep a measure of self-respect and the local shops had a degree of guaranteed business without which they could not have survived.

Wakes and Feasts

The Wakes Weeks (known in some parts of the West Riding as 'Feasts') were spread between June and August. The mills closed, the crowds left for the seaside and the town died for a week. Plans had been laid long before, money saved, special clothes bought and on the Friday night small boys would go to the railway sidings to see the special trains drawn up in readiness. Then on Saturday morning the streets would be alive, not with the usual streams of people making their way to the mills as on a working day (even a working Saturday morning in those days) but heading in one direction—to the station. By mid-afternoon the railway had moved thousands away to the delights of Blackpool, Morecambe, Scarborough and North Wales (and a few adventurous souls to Eastbourne or Torquay) and the town was deserted. The shops were closed, the mills were silent and even newspaper deliveries were suspended. The few—the very few—who stayed behind stocked up with food and sat out the week in a state of suspended animation.

The whole system had its logicality. A large textile mill could not be operated with reduced staff; so it was reasonable to close it completely. A regular pattern of town holidays—Rochdale one week, Oldham another, Todmorden another—meant that the seaside hotels and boarding houses could spread the load throughout the summer. But it also had its disadvantages—Blackpool in the third week in August was very much Rochdale-by-the-sea.

The Wakes Week has survived, although extended now to two weeks, even though the towns are no longer dominated by the textile industry. The older people still tend to refer to it by its traditional name, 'Rushbearing', recalling the time when new rushes were taken into the church. In many of the smaller Pennine towns the silence still reigns and shops still close and newspapers are still only available from a temporary sales point in the centre of the village. It is a less logical system now (and incomprehensible to the 'comers-in'), but it still spreads the load on the holiday resorts.

The autumn and winter brought a series of chapel 'Sings', which were occasions for the choir to give of its best in special services, all building up to the annual ritual of Handel's 'Messiah'. Churches (more often chapels) all over the North resounded to the oratorio week after week; soloists were at a premium and travelled round from choir to choir. If a major artiste were engaged it was essential to be at the chapel at least two hours before the advertised time to get any sort of seat at all; and major singers did take part in performances in the most unlikely places. Elsie Suddaby, Norman Allyn and Isobel Baillie were regular visitors to the Wesleyan Chapel in Littleborough and even a singer with only a local reputation could sing six or seven 'Messiah's' during the season. Most of them sang in most chapels in a very few years! The 'Messiah' survives, too, albeit fitfully, but it is still possible to hear it in most towns, and however the 'outsiders' may choose to perform it, the definitive performance so far as most Northerners are concerned is the one given by the Huddersfield Choral Society.

Even in the 1920s, though, chapel attendance was in decline and in 1932 the Methodist Circuits were rationalised. Many of the smaller chapels, often formed by a determined and zealous breakaway minority, were entirely reliant on the enthusiasm of a few individuals. Once they had gone, the whole organisation stagnated and then foundered. Patterns of life had changed also, and people were more aware and more critical of their surroundings, less willing to restrict themselves to chapel functions. Disillusion had come with the Great War, and in the twenties and thirties, horizons had broadened with travel, the cinema and radio. All the same, many of the remaining chapels have hung on and still inspire loyalty and affection for their own sake, rather than for what they represent.

Tiny chapels tucked away in remote places like Parrock Nook (above Rishworth) and Crimsworth Dean (on the old road between Hebden Bridge and Haworth) have adherents determined to keep them open in face of apparently insuperable difficulties. Crimsworth is typical—almost the archetypal moorland chapel. It traces its ancestry back to the 1740s, to Scotch Will Darney who set up the Crimsworth Dean Society. William Grimshaw brought the society to the notice of Wesley during the latter's visit of 1747 and the following year incorporated a visit to Crimsworth into his regular visit to the Haworth area.

The society met first in farmhouses, then in a barn, then finally in its own tiny chapel. At that time something like 400 people lived in the valley and the chapel was the natural centre for this scattered community. Now there are fewer than sixty and only about eight regular members of the congregation. Even

161

so, the chapel can count on many more for help. People who have moved away from the valley return for the anniversary services and around the area there is now a feeling that the worst times may be over for congregations like that at Crimsworth.

Relaxation and Radio

The Pennines were the playground of the local people during the pre-war years; hiking, cycling and even gliding were popular pastimes, and the regular rambles were a feature of every social group. The week was still governed by the mill-siren and 'the week' included Saturday mornings, but the weekend of a day and a half was full of local activities. League cricket flourished, Rugby League had its many enthusiasts and in 1928 Rochdale was the venue for an early speedway circuit. The towns had their theatres and even the villages had their cinemas. The North had its own film studios as well and a film history that went right back to the very earliest days. Films were shown in Holmfirth within a very few weeks of the first demonstration in this country in 1896 and soon afterwards imitation westerns were being made on the Pennines above the village. During the Boer War 'news-reel' shots of battles in South Africa were being faked in a public park in Blackburn!

Mancunian Films made shoe-string comedies in their studios in Dickenson Road and their films usually featured well-known Northern artistes like Norman Evans and Frank Randle. They were shot almost off-the-cuff and were rarely seen more than fifty miles from Manchester; but within the North they were sure to fill a cinema and formed part of the staple diet for every small-town film organisation. The studios survived until the mid-1950s when the building—significantly a derelict chapel—was taken over by the new giant of television.

In the 1930s, however, it was radio and the North had its own regional broadcasting network. The first transmitter had been at Trafford Park, but the coming of 2ZY Manchester and other studios in Leeds brought a new transmitter on the Pennines at Moorside Edge, just off the Huddersfield–Oldham road. The BBC's North Region flourished and became an integral part of Northern life besides providing more material for the national network than many other regions put together. The demise of regional radio is still regretted in the North and is seen by some as a deliberate attempt to 'formalise' radio under the direct control of an establishment based in London. Local radio, particularly the BBC's Blackburn station, has done much to keep the local traditions in writing alive, but the five BBC and IBA stations serving the Pennine area are seen as a poor substitute for what was, in effect, the 'voice' of the North as a whole.

1939–45

The 1939–45 War was less terrible than the Great War, although the blitzes of 1940 devastated the cities. Manchester lost its heart in a couple of fiery nights in 1941. The flames were clearly visible fifteen miles away and from the ridge of Blackstonedge the fires in Liverpool could be seen a clear fifty miles away. The Pennines had their bombs too, but the main memories of the wartime years are concerned with billetted soldiers and the arrival of the evacuees, first from the northern cities and later on from London. The arrival of the first group of children from Manchester produced one of Littleborough's legends. The women of the town had heard of the impending arrival and were at the station when the train pulled in. The children, all correctly labelled, were assembled, ready for the walk to a dispersal centre. The local people did not wait for that—they plucked children out of the crowd and, ignoring the protesting officials, simply took them home! The local 'grape-vine' eventually informed the harassed officials where the children were!

The Wakes Week became 'Holidays at Home', chapels became 'British Restaurants' with a full meal at a rock-bottom price, buses driven by an evil-smelling gas plant crawled up the hills (in some cases the passengers being forced to get off and walk behind) and in the last winter of the war a handful of V1s launched from under Heinkels dropped at Tottington and Royton. Mills which had closed in the Depression years became temporary barracks or service depots. Frankfort Mill, close by the canal in Littleborough, was crammed with (of all things) tea, producing the speculation that if a bomb got the mill there would be a strong brew all the way down the canal to Manchester.

The Aftermath

Then, hard on the heels of the peace, came the winter of 1947. The Pennines were used to severe winters (the first winter of the war had been a bad one with RAF convoys snowed up for days, one of them in the centre of Littleborough) but 1947 paralysed the trans-Pennine routes for weeks; 15ft, even 20ft, drifts were common, the railway was blocked and Lancashire was totally separated from Yorkshire for a while. Eventually the snow-ploughs got through from Rochdale to Littleborough and Little-borough to Todmorden and the old low-level route became a vital life-line between the counties. Some of the houses in the steep side-valleys were completely snowed-over and the ice on Hollingworth Lake was a foot and a half thick. There was to be nothing like that winter for years—thirty-two years to be precise!

The 'recovery' years after the war were characterised by the slogan 'Britain's Bread Hangs by Lancashire's Thread'. The mills, both cotton and wool, were booming, but by 1960 the first closures had come. Often it was simply a case of a natural decline, but in some instances—too many, it is suggested—local family-owned firms were simply bought out as part of a massive rationalisation on the part of larger firms. Regardless of their via-bility they were taken over in order to be closed—a classic exer-cise in asset-stripping. Many of the owning families took the opportunity to sell and get out—literally; Lancashire bore the brunt of this general decline and Yorkshire fared a little better. The families tended to hang on longer in the woollen industry, and even when they relinquished their hold often stayed on in the area and diversified into other industry.

As the traditional industries declined, the populations fell—in some cases disastrously. Todmorden lost a quarter of its popu-lation from its peak of 20,000; Littleborough, which had dropped from 12,000 to only a little over 10,000, was suddenly faced with 500 redundancies as one of its mills closed. Only adap-tability and natural resilience prevented whole towns from total collapse.

Only in the mid-1960s was the drift away from the North arrested and the position stabilised. It became obvious that the whole of the North was living in a post-revolutionary situation. The Industrial Revolution had been very much a battle and the signs of its devastation were all around. The statistics were daunting. There were thousands of acres of dereliction, unemployment was a constant nagging worry and the prospects for young people were uninspiring. There was more of one thing, and less of another, than in any other area. Rivers in the North were more polluted than rivers anywhere else, and head of the league table were the Roch and Irwell. (It was said that a small animal could walk across the surface of what was, in effect, a stream of sludge.) Bronchitis was endemic and industrial diseases brought about by working in the cotton and asbestos industries affected large percentages of every community. The overall quality of life was persistently lower in the North than anywhere else. A visiting officer from the Arts Council referred to Manchester as a cultural desert, and if one accepts that a desert is a place where things will not grow without fertilisation and irrigation, he was right. The local generators had run down; they needed overhauling and refuelling, but there seemed little chance of any help coming from within the North and the outside world seemed extraordinarily hard of hearing. For all their bright, permissive face, the Swinging Sixties did not seem to be swinging in the North's direction.

18
THE LAST SUPERLATIVE

Officially, the most recent Lancashire–Yorkshire link is simply the M62 which, since local government reorganisation in 1974, officially links the Metropolitan Counties of Merseyside, Greater Manchester and West Yorkshire to North Humberside. The Trans-Pennine Motorway, however, is engineering in the grand style, in the best traditions of the Rochdale Canal and the Manchester & Leeds Railway. Building the trans-Pennine section was by far the most difficult construction enterprise so far attempted in this country.

The motorway is garlanded with superlatives and near-superlatives. The Rakewood viaduct is the highest bridge in Lancashire (or, as it is now, in Greater Manchester); the Pennine Way foot-bridge over the motorway at Rockingstone Moss is the highest bridge above sea-level across a motorway in the country; Scammonden Bridge is the largest fixed-arch bridge in Britain (and possibly in Europe) and the 180ft cutting at Deanhead is the deepest rock road-cutting in Europe. Only the M6 and M62 climb to over 1,000ft above sea-level and nowhere else is a motorway carried across a dam embankment as the M62 is at Scammonden. Even the Worsley interchange down on the plain, where the M61, M62, M63, Salford Spur Motorway and East Lancashire Road meet, is unique. The Gravelly Hill Interchange in Birmingham is more complex a structure, but Worsley's junction is larger overall, links more roads—and at one point has the distinction of being seventeen lanes wide!

The Plan

The first proposals for the construction were made in 1961 and by 1964 the Ministry of Transport and the County Councils of Lancashire and the West Riding had agreed the line. During the planning discussions it was agreed that the motorway would be incorporated into the proposals to build a reservoir in the Scammonden valley—hence the 250ft high dam across the valley with the motorway running along the top of it. Work began in May 1968 and, although the cross-Pennine section was clearly the main task, spurs were also to be built from the motorway towards the northern edge of Manchester itself, to Bury and on to the existing motorway-standard road up the Irwell valley, to Rochdale and Oldham and, on the Yorkshire side, to Bradford and to Leeds.

The M62 would obviously be of great value. It would, in the words of the old canal prospectus, 'link the eastern and western seas' and reduce the cross-country journey from the best part of a working day to a matter of a couple of hours. It would cross both the M6 and the M1, would join Liverpool, Manchester, Bradford, Leeds and Hull and, with its ancillary routes, would bring towns like Bolton, Rochdale, Oldham, Halifax, Brighouse and Huddersfield into the motorway network. Importantly, it would give the Lancashire and Yorkshire conurbations a fast route to the Manchester International Airport.

The construction gangs (navvies in the best canal and railway tradition) moved in and began the monumental task of taking a six-lane highway over the Pennines. It was a job that was to outstrip all previous motorway constructions. The difficulties were enormous: on the Lancashire side allowance had to be made for possible mining subsidence all the way from Worsley to Milnrow and then the motorway had to be cut on as even a grade as possible to the top of the ridge. In many places (and not only on the moor) the peat was 20ft thick. Cuttings over 100ft deep had to be blasted through solid rock; wind speeds of up to 120mph had to be allowed for when building bridges; snow could be expected for six months of the year and up to 60in of rain a year anticipated.

Soon after leaving the Worsley interchange on its eastbound journey the motorway crossed the Irwell valley (and, incidentally, the old Manchester, Bolton and Bury Canal) and it was here that a highly unusual little local difficulty was encountered. Along the valley lies the Pendleton Fault which, with the Tunshill Fault south of Hollingworth Lake, makes the area less inherently 'stable' than most, so the Irwell valley bridge had to be built to resist the occasional movement along the geological fault-line. On 7 March 1972 an earth tremor which measured 4.4 on the Richter scale was experienced (and felt over a wide area from Preston to Leeds) without any effect on the bridge. Even this bridge had its place in the record books: unnoticed by the motorist as he drives over it, with a span of 200ft it is the largest single-span bridge in the old Lancashire county.

The motorway runs through the open country between the city of Manchester and the ring of old 'cotton' towns around its northern flank; at Besses o' th' Barn it passes under the Manchester–Bury railway, with the tracks supported on a curious reinforced concrete structure shaped rather like a flanged girder and separated by the 'fin' of the girder. Mining subsidence was considered to be a distinct possibility here, so the bridge was designed so that it could be adjusted to changes in ground-level.

The Pennine Crossing

Beyond here, the Lancashire spur of the Pennines is very evident, curving round ahead to join the main bulk in a seemingly unbroken line, but even here, on a clear day, the White House at the top of Blackstonedge can quite clearly be seen. The scenery has been likened, unfairly perhaps, to a Lowry painting. The distant mill chimneys are certainly there, but so are the tower blocks and trading estates, all set against the backdrop of the hills.

For a short distance, the motorway obliterates the old Heywood arm of the Rochdale Canal; then it dips to pass first under the old railway, then over the canal (both of them trans-Pennine pioneers) before reaching the exit at Milnrow at the foot of the Pennine ascent. Here the motorway is roughly 500ft above sea-level with over 700ft to go before it reaches its summit at Rockingstone Moss.

It was between here and Scammoden that the major obstacles were met. First comes a cutting nearly 50ft deep, then a substantial embankment, then another cutting to bring the road directly out on to the Rakewood viaduct over the Longdenend valley. This has four main spans of 150ft and two end spans of 120ft and the maximum height above the valley is over 140ft. Severe cross-winds can be experienced on the viaduct and in this exposed location substantial temperature variations can be expected; so joints have been incorporated at the western end to allow for expansion.

The Rakewood viaduct is, like so many of the massive constructions on the M62, a surprisingly elegant structure. The splendid scenery in this area would have been ruined by an unsympathetic structure, but the simple, apparently slim lines of the viaduct positively enhance the scene. Hollingworth Lake lies just below the viaduct and it is now an integral part of the backdrop to the lake. When the motorway was opened the authorities (much to the surprise of the local people) proudly floodlit the bridge and it provided a dramatic view—an elegant pale turquoise against the deep velvety black of the hills.

The motorway then climbs steeply, curving along the shoulder of the moor with the wild and desolate Longdenend valley to the right. This is the Pennines at their most typical— the scene includes one of the earliest water-powered mills, far below in the valley, seemingly utterly remote from any habitation, and the remains of three ancient farmsteads (the one furthest up the valley well over 1,000ft up yet shielded from the worst of the weather by the enfolding valley-sides).

The Windy Hill cutting through which the motorway now runs is 120ft deep, cut through rock and designed to keep the road below the level of the prevailing cloud. Extra-large drainage channels have been cut in this area to take the heavy run-off of water from the moor. Here too are the two plaques, one on each side of the road, which mark the old county boundary between Lancashire and Yorkshire.

The Pennine Way crosses the motorway just beyond the boundary and its foot-bridge is, again, an elegant feature. An underpass would have been possible—and perhaps cheaper— and it is a tribute to the motorway designers that they chose to build this slim cat-walk 65ft above the roadway. Even this bridge had to be built to withstand the severe weather conditions and the parabolic arch which springs over 200ft across the motorway has its legs splayed slightly to allow for the moortop winds. Again, the designers allowed for up to 120mph.

Appropriately, this is Windy Hill, the sharp ridge between

Lancashire and Yorkshire where—it has been suggested—Daniel Defoe found himself wandering in a blizzard in August. Snow in August is, admittedly, highly unusual, but it is more than usual to experience snow between November and May, so much research was done before the actual profile of the motorway here was settled. Models of the main motorway features were made at the National Physical Laboratory and imitation snow—in fact powdered balsa wood—was blown around and across in an attempt to discover the effect.

Rockingstones

At Rockingstones Moss the M62 crosses the A672 at what must be the most desolate interchange in the country. Yet only a few yards away is the Windy Hill television repeater station, which is a vital link in the country's microwave communications network.

Then between here and Deanhead, where the motorway cuts a swinging curve through the ridge between the Ryburn and Scammonden valleys, the two carriage-ways are separated by a considerable distance. Yet even here, civilisation is not entirely absent. Between the two carriage-ways nestles a farm and across the valley is the old Derby Bar coaching inn, now a sophisticated nightspot and renamed 'Exit 22' after the Rockingstones interchange! Just above the inn is a solid Victorian house; this was once Lord Savile's hunting lodge and it is now another popular restaurant.

The peat covering on the moor was up to 20ft deep and it was found that the only way to remove it was to dig a vertical shaft and then excavate horizontally (excavators working on the surface sank immediately). Well over 60in of rain fell in one year (and 12in in one month), turning the whole area into a quagmire. One of the engineers remarked that it was the only place he had ever worked where it actually rained upwards! In cloud, visibility was practically nil and the temperature could be anything up to 6°F colder than at the lower levels. This, plus the wind and swirling cloud, made severe exposure a real danger and frostbite also occurs under these conditions.

170

Scammonden

The Deanhead cutting was the next major obstacle. Ten excavators, each capable of cutting 25,000 cubic yards per week, were used, feeding a fleet of trucks, some of which were capable of taking away 45 tons of rock-spoil per load. At its deepest, the sides of the cutting rise 180ft, and across it arches the Scammonden Bridge carrying the A6025 Elland–Denshaw road. The scaffolding for the bridge arch used up 70 *miles* of steel tubing and in the depths of winter it was coated with 1,000 tons of ice. The statistics are impressive. The arch is 410ft across and the roadway 120ft above the motorway and, with its approach spans, the bridge is nearly 700ft from end to end. But once again, it is an elegant structure curving gracefully high above the speeding traffic of the motorway. In cloudy conditions, indeed, the arch curves up into the mist, obscuring the full height of the cutting. The road across the bridge was kept open during its construction with a diversion at the actual site of the bridge. This involved traffic inching slowly down a precipitous 1 in 4 track to the level of the motorway, across its foundations, then up to the moor level again (by a steep lane). The view of the operations, passengers said, was tremendous, but the driver, if wise, did not look!

Once through the cutting, the motorway immediately crosses the dam holding back the waters of the Scammonden reservoir. Once again, this is a massive construction—2,000ft long and 250ft high, holding back 1,700 million gallons of water. The clay core alone took three years to construct and there are elaborate safety precautions. Within the dam are sensitive gauges which can detect a movement of as little as 0.02 of an inch and downstream is an instrument which, by means of light returned from special reflectors on the dam's face, can measure changes in distance up to an accuracy of one part in one million.

The reservoir at Scammonden is only part of a larger catchment scheme. Water from the adjoining Colne valley is fed into the reservoir here by way of a 1¾ mile tunnel through the ridge separating the valleys. The catchment area is capable of supplying up to 9 million gallons a day to the reservoir. There is seldom any shortage of water on the high moor, as the motorway's engineers discovered!

Beyond the dam the motorway curves through yet another cutting, passes under the A62 trans-Pennine road and reaches the next interchange at the edge of Huddersfield. Even here it is not quite an 'ordinary' road; it runs high on the ridge with wide, sweeping views of the towns away to the North. Then it plunges down into the Calder valley, only to rise again and swing away towards Bradford and Leeds. From Milnrow to Outlane, near Huddersfield (Exits 21 to 23) is only about 10 miles, but that 10 miles must surely be the most consummate example of the modern engineer's skill anywhere in the country, and the equal of anything in the world. To use the Trans-Pennine Motorway for the first time is, to say the least, exhilarating and even when used regularly, it never ceases to excite. One can find it benign or swept by battering wind and rain, mist-shrouded or sparkling under a huge arch of cloudless sky. One can be swept along, the moor seeming to leap away to either side, or have the feeling of fighting every inch of the way against a howling gale. It is possible, indeed, to drive up through low cloud to find the top section clear under the stars. By day the traffic thunders across (it is among the most heavily used motorways in the country) but the best way to appreciate its true majesty is probably by night—the line of lights swings away across the flat, black face of the moor, showing the true scale of the whole construction, and the road seems to sing under the wheels. Not surprisingly, perhaps, the M62 tends to silence unwanted conversation, if the wind does not. Then, far away and below, the intricate pattern of civilisation's lighted streets appears and the descent is like coming into an airport.

19
A PENNINE IDENTITY

The coming of the Trans-Pennine Motorway did not produce the same great changes as did the coming of the canal and railway. Rather it coincided with some important (indeed, traumatic) changes in the fortunes of the North. Its very existence prompted the construction of the appropriately named Trans-Pennine Trading Estate in Rochdale and the general development of housing, particularly on the Lancashire side. A number of major companies have established distribution centres on the estate in Rochdale, which is within a few yards of the spur leading to the M62. Significantly, it is also within a few yards of the Manchester–Bradford railway line (but without a link to it!). In fact the estate fills the strip of land between the railway and the Rochdale canal and is bisected by a lane which passes over March Barn Bridge. It is a surrealist situation. The bridge was designed by Rennie (and, it has been said, was designed as an experiment). It crosses the canal at a slight angle and is now acknowledged as the world's first skew bridge. The bridge sits placidly alongside the trading estate and is an officially designated Ancient Monument no less, restored with help from a major oil company!

Changing Patterns

A tide of new housing (much of it badly sited and totally out of character with the area) laps against the Pennine foothills above Rochdale. Milnrow and Littleborough (both 'convenient for Motorway') have felt the full impact of this development. Twenty-five per cent of Littleborough's population is housed on the estates built since 1968 and after the disastrous fall in population from 12,000 to about 10,000 it is now, at something over 13,000, bigger than it ever was. It is also relatively younger, since the 'comers-in' were mainly first-time buyers, often with small children. This expansion put tremendous pressures on local services and, unfortunately, coincided with local government changes which diluted effective local power. Both the Greater Manchester County and the new Boroughs within it were essentially urban concepts and the boroughs in particular paid scant attention to their rural fringes.

Admittedly, the old Lancashire cotton towns had enormous problems: the traditional industries continued to decline; a large proportion of the housing in the towns was well past its effective life; social and environmental problems abounded. Eventually, the whole area was granted Intermediate Area status, which guaranteed a certain, but limited, amount of government aid. This was only partially effective in attracting new industry: faced with the alternatives of a brand-new factory on a green-field site in an area like Merseyside (which had full development status) or a restricted site in one of the old cotton towns with only limited government aid, it is not surprising that much development went to Merseyside. Again, the old towns failed to provide for 'headquarters' staff (one multi-national, looking for office accommodation, could find no suitable building north of Manchester), so effective control of local industry was lost. This led to a general imbalance with too many low-paid unskilled jobs and too few real career prospects. Fifty years ago it was perfectly possible for a young man to start at the bottom in the textile industry and finish off as an executive, without leaving his original mill. This was no longer possible.

The Yorkshire Pennines and Calderdale in particular had other problems. The woollen industry survived better than cotton, but, for instance, the sheer lack of level ground in Calderdale made it impossible to attract either new industry or large-scale new housing. Once again, with local government reorganisation, control was felt to be remote—in some cases very remote indeed. The sudden pool of unemployed school-leavers in 1976 prompted the Job Creation Programme; clearly the problem areas like Rochdale and Calderdale could make good use of the substantial finance available. But only schemes under £60,000 could be agreed locally—schemes involving over that figure had to be sanctioned by national headquarters in London.

It is not surprising that the problems of the 1970s brought about an increasing awareness of what came to be known as the 'Pennine Identity'. The influx of new residents had brought about a definite growth of interest in the area, all kinds of societies flourished and amenity and environmental groups were particularly active. In 1972, Calder Civic Trust, based in Hebden Bridge, issued a report suggesting that the South Pennines were, amongst other things, ideally suited for recreation, and that this might be a partial solution to the problems brought about by the decline of the traditional industries. Other groups responded with similar proposals and this led to the setting up of the Pennine Park Association, which drew its strength from the various environmental and recreational groups and had the declared aim of having the South Pennines designated and developed as a regional 'park' bridging the gap between the Peak National Park and the Yorkshire Dales National Park. The local authorities responded by setting up a parallel organisation, SCOSPA—the Standing Conference of South Pennine Authorities.

Conservation

The authorities began to recognise the value of the Pennine area. Greater Manchester Council, for instance, set out a specific strategy for the improvement of river valleys and this led to environmental schemes to enhance the Tame and Croal valleys. Again, these could be only partially effective since massive amounts of money (an estimated £20 million a year) would be needed to clean the rivers flowing through those valleys.

Much conservation—official and unofficial—has taken place in the Pennines during the 1970s. The old centre of Ripponden is a Conservation Area; a museum at Golcar, in the Colne valley, is housed in a fine three-storey hand-loom weaver's cottage; the Pioneers' Store in Rochdale is the centre-piece of another conservation area, which carefully recreates the street scene of the mid-nineteenth century and the town's museum is now housed in the Georgian vicarage alongside the parish church. Such projects would have been inconceivable ten years before; slowly, the unique heritage of the area was being rediscovered and protected.

Inexpensive housing first attracted the outsiders to the Pennine towns and villages and among the cheapest houses were the old cottages, which, a few short years ago, were considered to be slums and fit only for demolition. The discerning recognised the potential of these buildings and many of the old upland weaving hamlets, once virtually derelict, are now among the most desirable places to live. Even the mid-Victorian terraced houses are in demand for their sheer convenience and the lowly back-to-back (the true back-to-back—houses facing both ways with a central party wall along the terrace) can provide a living room and small kitchen, bathroom and two small bedrooms (and therefore adequate accommodation for a single person or a young couple looking for the cheapest way to start a home). Sheep farming is still very much part of the Pennine way of life, and the leasing of additional grazing land has meant that many surplus (or perhaps derelict) farms and barns came on to the market.

Stone cleaning has revealed that the local millstone grit was not, as had been assumed, black, but a pale honey-gold which glowed in the clearer post-Industrial Revolution light. The decline of industry has eradicated the once all-enveloping smoke-pall, colour has come back to hills that were once literally soot-crusted and, in effect, the climate has changed. Less smoke means more sun and clearer skies, which in turn means a more rapid development of plant life—gardens blaze with flowers which a few years ago would simply not have grown. And the end of industrialisation has meant that the countryside has crept back; the valleys are taking on the appearance they had a hundred and fifty years ago.

Visitors and Tourists

Already the South Pennines are an expanding recreational area. Hollingworth Lake, which was once in decline as a leisure venue, is now a Country Park with formal and informal facilities, upgraded services and car-parks, picnic areas and an information centre. Much of the park was created from a derelict refuse tip which scarred the eastern side of the lake. The lake has contrasting faces—sailing, rowing (even wind-surfing) on its surface, a nature reserve and yet pubs and cafes around the edge! The visitors now come in their thousands all the year round and many, after their first visit, use it as a jumping-off point to explore the surrounding area.

The Pennine Way, now heavily tramped, runs through the whole area and the Calderdale Way rings the Calder valley. The Water Authorities have opened up more and more of their catchment land; hang-gliders sweep away from the slopes of Blackstonedge and Brown Wardle Hill; walkers, strollers and ramblers rediscover the old half-hidden pack-horse roads; canoes glide along the clear surface of the once 'long, black' line of the canal; and horses are everywhere! The Worth valley railway takes thousands more up and down the valley, cars cluster round every convenient viewpoint and parade slowly along the sky-line roads.

Tourism is a growth industry in the South Pennines, as it is in so many other places, and much of the interest has been stimulated by West Yorkshire Council's tourist information service, now known more correctly as the South Pennine Tourist Information Service. The pundits tended to smile condescendingly behind their hands when a Tourist Information Centre was set up in Hebden Bridge, but the centre and its services have proved a resounding success and much of the 'awareness' stems from the fact that the information centres at Hebden Bridge and Haworth exist. In making information available to the visitor these centres have also informed the local resident.

The metamorphosis is particularly apparent in Hebden Bridge. Traditionally, people who made their homes in this tumbling town of stacked houses and precipitous streets were considered to be decidedly peculiar—unbalanced in personality as their town is unbalanced physically. Now, Hebden Bridge proclaims itself 'The Pennine Centre' and no one quarrels with the definition.

Nutclough Mill

Campaign for the North, the sturdy devolutionist movement, has its home at Hebden Bridge, as has the Pennine Development Trust, supported by charitable trusts and breathing life into various Pennine ventures. The Trust is the logical outcome of the awareness of the problems facing the Pennines—it aims to create a better understanding of the area, to strengthen the 'Pennine Identity' through social, cultural and recreational activity and it is hoped that it will stem the continued drift away from the area by widening the range of occupational opportunities.

One of the first projects to be tackled by the Trust is the renovation and restoring to use of Nutclough Mill, close by the Keighley road in Hebden Bridge. The mill itself is a symbolic and emotive object. It is the one-time home of an early cooperative of fustian manufacturers and producers of ready-made clothing (products for which Hebden Bridge became well known).

In 1870, a group of local fustian cutters formed the Hebden Bridge Fustian Manufacturing Co-operative Society. Christian Socialism played a part in its concept and, indeed, some of its members had been involved with the Chartist Movement in former days. By 1873, 24 people were employed and the movement took over Nutclough, which was followed by a small mill. By 1880 it employed 260 people and by 1900, 356, and the mill had been greatly extended. Members of the society played a leading part in the setting up of the Co-operative Productive Federation in 1882 and in the Labour Co-operative Association in 1884. From 1882 the society also promoted a series of university extension lectures, which were given free in the largest hall in the town. From this beginning, Robert Halstead, former weaver and a member of the society, joined Albert Mansbridge in founding the Workers' Educational Association. Dr Cosmo Lang, later Archbishop of Canterbury, was one of the visiting lecturers and often paid tribute to the 'tough-headed and warm-hearted brethren of the North, especially . . . the heroic little company which was for so many years a witness of all that was truest and best in co-operation—the fustian manufacturers of Hebden Bridge'.

So many of the threads that went to make the North can be drawn together at Nutclough Mill and its very existence now is typical of the problems facing the area. Appropriately (and symbolically) the trust dedicated to its restoration, as well as Campaign for the North, the Pennine Park Association and the Pennine's own magazine, are all based in the converted Birchcliffe chapel.

The tradition of self-help has always been strong in the Pennines and the objectives of organisations like the Pennine Development Trust are the logical continuation of this tradition. Nonconformism grew within the homes of the upland villagers whilst the Established Church stagnated. The Rochdale Canal was conceived by separate groups of local men who came together to fight the long battle to build it and it was local people who first proposed its restoration, rather than any national pressure group. The canal was originally built in recognition of a local need and the restoration project recognises the same need translated now to the context of tourism, the Pennine Park and the need to improve the general quality of local life.

Substantial industrial empires could trace their ancestry back, through one family, to a hand-loom weaver working in one of the old villages. Gordon Harvey was an enlightened mill-owner, Internationalist, Member of Parliament and an idealist fifty years ahead of his time, yet he was instrumental in setting up the (as it seemed then) curiously named 'Beautiful Littleborough Society'. Founded in 1919, this pioneer environmental group looked to the future by planting trees (which have given Littleborough an unusual 'green heart') and commemorated the past through a series of lectures, many of them given by one of the overlookers from Harvey's own mill. The information contained in Fred Jackson's lecture notes provides one of the few reliable links with the area's past. As a local man, he could draw on spoken recollection going back a hundred years or more and his notes are a valuable source of 'colour' for present-day historians. The present-day Civic Trust in Littleborough acknowledges the debt it owes to Harvey, Jackson and the pioneer society.

The Co-operative movement, exemplified by the Rochdale Pioneers and the fustian weavers of Nutclough, spread outwards from the Pennines to form its own vast trading empire and diversified into Christian Socialism and the WEA.

The Calderdale Way

The Calderdale Way is one of the more recent examples of the development of a local idea—in this case by the Civic Trusts of Brighouse, Elland, Halifax, Ryburn and Calder, Civic Societies in Sowerby Bridge and Shelf and Todmorden Conservation Group. A list of the objectives of the Calderdale Way Association might almost be taken as a statement of intent for the various groups sponsoring the Pennine Identity. The Calderdale Way Association declared that it aimed to:

> Stimulate a greater awareness and concern for our landscape and architectural heritage and the need for continuity as well as change.
>
> Initiate more positive co-operation between voluntary, statutory and landowning interests to achieve environmental improvement.
>
> Encourage in young people a spirit of adventure ... tempered by respect for working landscapes and wild life habitats.
>
> Inspire artist and naturalist, poet and historian, photographer and creative writer to use their talent in further interpretation of the area.
>
> Ultimately dispel [sic] the wasteland image of the industrial north by demonstrating that in its bleakness lies a beauty that is found along the Way.

The work of delineating the path started as a collaborative venture among the voluntary bodies in 1973 and a draft text already existed when, in 1976, the Countryside Commission outlined its new policy of Recreation Footpaths, placing more emphasis on 'well publicised, signed and waymarked routes in the green belt and urban fringe near major towns, to improve opportunities for the great majority of visitors to the countryside who do not walk long distances or spend more than one day on a walk'. This drew a statutory body into the scheme; the County Council's countryside officer for the area became involved and the work on bringing some sections of the pathway up to standard was achieved through the Job Creation Programme. From an initial idea in the minds of local enthusiasts has come a major amenity for the Calderdale area.

The Way describes a fifty mile circuit round the new Borough of Calderdale and is adequately waymarked and provided with link paths to bus and rail connections. Taking it (and thousands have since its opening in 1978), the walker is led, by way of some spectacular scenery, through the unique blend of history that is special to the Pennines. From the southern outskirts of Halifax it runs over the shoulder of the moor and down the precipitous old track to Ripponden (deeply set in the Ryburn valley), then up by way of Mill Bank (one of the most attractive of the upland villages) and out over the hills again to drop down to Cragg Vale with its shadowy memories of the Coiners who murdered, were finally run to earth and were hanged at York. From here it heads for the high moor by way of one of the old tracks which crosses the Pennine Way at Withen Gate, near Stoodley Pike and 1,200ft up, with a vast panorama of tumbled moor and tiny farms, the valley towns seeming far, far below.

The Way heads now for Lumbutts and, looking down from the heights, the walker might well reflect that not all that long ago workers heading for the mill at Lumbutts walked this way in the early morning. They could be seen from below—a line of flickering candles making their way slowly down the moor, the mill bell speeding their step.

At Lumbutts is the water tower which once held three water-wheels one on top of the other, fed by syphoning water from a series of dams. (This is ample evidence of the importance of water power in the early days of the Industrial Revolution.) Then the way drops to Todmorden and the busy valley road and railway. But it drops by way of the Quaker burial ground, the Unitarian church and the memories of 'Honest John' Fielden. It climbs again over the shoulder of Todmorden Edge (still, it seems, echoing to the rhetoric of Wesley) to drop once more to cross the Cliviger Gorge, only to climb again to swing east above Cross Stone Church. Then it comes to Blackshaw Head on the Long Causeway and carries on to Heptonstall:

> Blackshawhead for travellers,
> Heptonstall for Trust.

An ideal defensive position, it was fortified during the war between Royalists and Parliamentarians. Its defenders found that they could conveniently roll rocks down on the heads of the attackers! From Heptonstall it is down again, into the densely wooded Hebden Water valley and Hardcastle Crags with Crimsworth Dean reaching away to the north, to the old pack-horse road over to Haworth. Then it is up again, to Pecket Well, a cluster of old weavers' cottages and some much older, reaching back to the fifteenth century; then a curve up and round to emerge high above the Calder valley again. Scout Rock and Crow Hill at Sowerby dominate Mytholmroyd and, just along the valley, is Luddendenfoot where Branwell Brontë was clerk at the station. Off the track goes again, down into Luddenden Dean, then up and up by way of Saltonstall and Wainstalls to Hunter Hill, one of the highest points on the Way and the site of a Civil War battle at Slaughter Gap where the Parliamentarians were defeated in January 1644.

The Way swings round again, skirting the northern edge of Halifax, runs by way of Holdsworth House (built in 1633 on land which once belonged to the Knights of St John of Jerusalem) then on to Shelf, down into the sheltered Shibden valley and on towards Brighouse.

Here, at the eastern end of Calderdale, is the country of the railway viaduct and the navigation. The arteries feed the manufactories in the hills and take their finished goods to the world outside the Pennines. Brighouse itself is largely a product of the Industrial Revolution, yet Elland (once the key town in the Halifax parish with a charter dating back to 1317) stands just to one side and Kirklees Priory (where Robin Hood died) to the other.

The Calderdale Way is unique, but its features are not. The pattern of moorland village and early industrial town, navigation and railway, the mixture of primeval and man-made, an industrial history laid over a skeleton of older—even legendary—times, is a phenomenon repeated over and over again in the Pennines. It has been called a 'hidden heritage' and it is only now that the very special history of the area is being discovered and interpreted. Significantly, it is the people living in the hills, natives and newcomers, who are in the forefront of this movement—probing, researching, literally digging out a history that is uniquely their own.

EPILOGUE: AND STILL
THE HILLS REMAIN

To travel into the Pennines is to be immediately aware of contrast and change. The motorway sweeps towards the hills past new complexes of anonymous warehousing and sprawling estates of equally anonymous instant neighbourhoods imagining themselves to be, if not Shangri-La, at least a close approximation to Beverly Hills. The North has always been more classless than the South (and most other places as well). It grew from nothing, unhampered (and yet unaided) by the squirearchy, has constantly changed and adapted, contracted, improvised and expanded as the circumstances of 200 years demanded. The North feels at home in this new age; the one-level society doggedly pursued by generations of preachers and politicians, writers and comics has produced a people determined (sometimes grimly determined) to make the most of what life has to offer—at last.

This is a restless, volatile society, which is yet amiable, casual and comfortable. Life, for all its problems, is no longer a desperate struggle a hairbreadth away from starvation, a cock-stride away from the insistent mill-siren. Life is easier here—less hedged about with imposed convention—than in most places. The Great Outdoors (a great deal of it) is on your doorstep and the Pennines are a playground just up the road. Old coaching inns and carters' rests glitter with light and echo with music; there's wind-surfing and hang-gliding, walking, horse-riding and motorcycle scrambling—and Egg Foo-Yung from the corner on the way home.

Yet this is in the foreground. Behind it all is the legacy of industrialism. 'Textile Industry Collapse Alert' runs the headline in the local newspaper. 6,256 textile workers in the North West lost their jobs in three months in 1979. Rochdale counts itself lucky that it only lost 400 of them. Employers give the industry a maximum life of ten years, the trade unions a mere five. Turkey has sent 4,835 tonnes of yarn to Britain where the limit should be 2,949 tonnes, and the problem is not confined to cotton yarn. In

1977 the import of man-made fibre tufted carpets from the USA was 132 tonnes, while in the first nine months alone of 1979 it was 6,570 tonnes. Imports of polyester textured yarn were 150 tonnes in 1977, while the first nine months of 1979 saw 4,376 tonnes come in. An experienced textile worker sniffs the air and senses that he will be without his job in a handful of years—for a man of fifty this means retirement. A small, hard core of unemployment is a built-in feature of the textile town economy. The images change as the towns adapt—Manchester is now computers and aircraft with hardly a bale of cotton fabric to be seen, but it is no longer the bustling, brassy Cottonopolis.

Victoria station has a bright new face, but the Lancashire & Yorkshire Railway is long gone. The old main line to Yorkshire has been down-graded and the short diesel multiple units wail balefully as they start the long climb towards the hills. Newton Heath and Middleton Junction are gone, and Rochdale station has been rebuilt, but is now only a third the size it was and without the distinctive paraphernalia of the 1880s heyday. There are no trains to Bury and Bolton now, and the Bacup branch is virtually obliterated.

The town Rochdale itself keeps some of its graceful centre, but is dominated by tower blocks and a new shopping centre which clings to the sharp slope of the valley. Consumers, rather than customers, make their way from the huge plasticated bus station down escalators, up escalators and across covered walkways to the shopping centre. Even the old open market is covered now and the stall-holders stand in their yellow plastic boxes like so many Aunt Sallys. The focus of the shopping centre is the Place Tourcoing (named after one of Rochdale's twin-towns) and the way out is by way of the Bielefeld Brücke across Newgate. Walking this way, one walks over the site of the Old Clock Face pub, haunt of dialect enthusiasts since the days of Edwin Waugh; some say one walks over Rochdale's soul as well. The old Pioneers' Store is behind the shopping centre, while the new one rises alongside, as slick and luxurious a store as any anywhere.

The town has made massive efforts, by way of pioneering methods, to improve its environment and has met with middling success. It wins awards for its schemes, but worries about their economic value. Its town hall now houses a council responsible for over 200,000 people in the new Metropolitan Borough stretching from the Manchester suburbs to the heights of Blackstonedge, from the burgeoning gardens of the Edgar Woodism of Alkrington Garden Suburb to the remote fastness of the moor-top farm, taking in the tower blocks, the Country Park, Pennine Drive and Norford Way, the Community-based Action Areas, crumbling terraces and acres of dereliction on the way. Significantly, some would say, its civic theatre is named after its most famous daughter, Gracie Fields, rather than its most famous son, John Bright.

Littleborough, hemmed in by the hills, still retains its character; the toll-house still stands at the junction of the Halifax and Todmorden turnpikes; the trans-Pennine routes fan out from its centre (roads old and new over Blackstonedge, dominant to the east, and roads, canal and railway northwards towards the Summit Pass). There have been massive changes here too. Virtually no natural fibre is woven now. Littleborough means chemicals and pharmaceuticals, plastic portable buildings and the inevitable industrial estate. 'Cleggs' and 'Laws' are gone and Fothergill & Harvey have gone over to plastic-coated fabrics and carbon fibre. And the pickles that grace the counters of the most elegant shops in London are made here! Great wedges of new housing jab at the old village from the south and boutiques, delicatessen and antique shops stand side by side with the old established businesses. But the changes have been slotted into the old way of doing things and the town's personality remains. An hour's gentle stroll takes the walker from the town square by way of the first trans-Pennine canal and railway, the pack-horse and turnpike road all the way through the early, gentler industrial revolution (through signs of both what it brought and what it destroyed for ever) back to the square again. Twenty minutes takes one to bustling, breezy Hollingworth Lake, and another hour to the heights of Blackstonedge.

The surprising thing is that so much of the old North remains, that so much has stayed to be rediscovered. Reddyshore Scoutgate still rims the western edge of the Summit Pass and the valley still carries road, railway and canal through to Todmorden. But now the cables of the electricity grid leap across the gap and higher still is a major aircraft flight-path.

Todmorden crouches between its hills, still straddling the now imaginary border between Lancashire and Yorkshire. The Old Hall is a fine restaurant and the town hall, cleaned and gleaming, is the finest memorial to a still proud and independent town. The changes have been fewer in Todmorden; it is just that little bit further into the hills, that little bit further from Manchester and Leeds. It has escaped the worst excesses of 'plaquitat' development but has not yet completely taken hold of a new role in Pennine life. It remains one of the most underrated towns in the north, busy with its own life, its operatic, antiquarian, angling and conservation societies—altogether a determinedly self-sufficient town.

Hebden Bridge looks both ways with confidence. Heptonstall, old and unchanging, dreams from the top of one crag; the Birchcliffe Centre clings to another, busy with ideas of expanding the Pennine Identity and devolution. In between stands the Information Centre with its tourists wading through the deluge of local publications, maps and guides. A once derelict mill now houses restaurant, boutiques and craft workshops, and antique shops abound. The steep streets are alive with visitors seeking that hidden heritage and just over the hill Haworth bares its heritage for the world to see.

The ghost of the eighteenth-century coiner 'King' David Hartley still haunts Cragg Vale, Mytholmroyd still tailors riding kit and keeps its station atop a high, cleaned arch. Old Sowerby still looks down from its tongue of land—Sowerby Bridge to one side, the deeply wooded Ryburn to the other. Halifax has rediscovered its Piece Hall and, with it, much of the handsomeness that makes Halifax a better than average town. It shows off its handsome buildings by way of a Town Trail and does not fail to include the space-age headquarters of its building society—a structure that seems poised to take off from the steep Halifax hillside. Space-age it may be now, but the roots of this and every other building society go deep into the ideal of mutual and equitable co-operation.

To the north still lies Saltaire, representative of all that was benevolent, and Top Withens, gale-lashed and remote, still hears Cathy calling for her Heathcliff. To the south, Hudders-

field vies with Halifax in providing a ring-road round its heart
that is balletic as well as utilitarian! The Colne valley pushes up
into the hills to Standedge, Marsden and Saddleworth; the opposite sides of the ridge are commuter territory now. The Pennine
Way walker on his way from Edale to the Cheviots looks down
from the ridge between. Ashton, Stalybridge and Mossley have
come together into Tameside; Oldham, high on its hill, still
sprouts a forest of mill chimneys but has built itself a splendid
civic centre—and retained Tommyfield, the epitome of open
markets.

The Pennines were never totally Lancashire nor wholly Yorkshire, and even Cheshire claimed a portion. Saddleworth, for all
that it lay firmly on the western slopes, was in the West Riding;
the A672 road from Oldham went into Yorkshire, out again and
in again before it even reached the crest of the moor. Todmorden
had been literally bisected by the county boundary until the
1880s, when it was moved south to coincide with the Littleborough Urban District boundary at Steanorbottom. Yet Todmorden kept its postal address as Todmorden, Lancashire, to the
confusion of all concerned.

Reorganisation

Local government reorganisation in 1973 put the South Pennines into five counties. The inconceivable happened—
Yorkshire was divided into North, West and South (and the East
Riding around Hull became part of Humberside and Yorkshire
south of the Tees became Cleveland). Lancashire was carved up
into three. The new Lancashire stopped at the Rossendale Fells
where Greater Manchester took over. (Merseyside was formed
around Liverpool; Lancashire took over land, Yorkshire land,
north of the Ribble and lost Warrington to Cheshire!) However
rational the reorganisation might be, it was seen as a takeover at
the local level and an imposition of authority from outside. On
both counts it was thoroughly resented.

There was no logical name for the new county based on Man-
chester and the working title 'South-East Lancashire–North-
East Cheshire' was adopted. Mercifully, this was shortened to
SELNEC which prompted one Saddleworth notable, saddened at

the thought of the impending takeover to remark, 'I don't like th' idea of goin' in wi' Oldham, I don't like th' idea of leavin' Yorkshire. But I'll be buggered if I'll be tekken over bi a set of bloody *initials*!' SELNEC was dropped in favour of Greater Manchester—GMC for short. The new counties were perhaps logical administratively, but emotionally—particularly in the case of Greater Manchester—they were anathema to the local people. Mancunians have never considered themselves to be Lancastrians (even if they lived in Stretford which was 'Lancashire' up to 1973 and where both Lancashire County Cricket and Manchester United played). Similarly, Lancastrians had never looked on Manchester as their mother city. It was the nearest big city, shopping centre, even regional capital, but not spiritual home.

The once proudly independent County Boroughs resented an imposed County level of government almost as much as the Urban Districts resented the amalgamation into (some would say takeover by) the big towns which formed Greater Manchester's ten Metropolitan Boroughs. Worst of all, most of the new boroughs took the name of the biggest of the old towns. Saddleworth had to call itself 'Oldham', Littleborough gritted its teeth and agreed that, officially at least, it was 'Rochdale'. Ramsbottom disappeared altogether, split between Bury and Rossendale, Greater Manchester and Lancashire. Such carving-up would be unfortunate anywhere, but it was felt particularly deeply in Lancashire and Yorkshire (used, as they were, to settling their own affairs in their own way) and huge barriers of resentment arose. Yorkshire handled things slightly better, at least psychologically. The borough based on Huddersfield became 'Kirklees' and Brighouse, Shelf, Halifax, Ripponden, Hebden Bridge and Todmorden became 'Calderdale'. Keighley, on the other hand, became 'Bradford'—as did Haworth!

Greater Manchester Police arrived, as did West Yorkshire, but North West Gas remained. Buses became GMT or West Yorkshire Metro, and they subsidised both ends of the old Lancashire & Yorkshire main line. But British Rail hung on to the middle section—and administered it from Preston! The Post Office ignored the whole reorganisation: Rochdale is still

Rochdale, Lancs, and Littleborough's postal address is Littleborough, Lancs, even though it is now part of Rochdale which is in Greater Manchester, not Lancashire. Whitworth's correct postal address is Whitworth, Rochdale, Lancs. Whitworth is in Lancashire—part of the borough of Rossendale—but Rochdale is not. It is in Greater Manchester. The postal code for Littleborough and Rochdale is OL, which stands for Oldham—an entirely different Metropolitan Borough, albeit in Greater Manchester. OL is also used for Todmorden, which is in an entirely different county; unless you happen to be the Post Office, in which case it is still in Lancashire (which it hasn't been for nearly a hundred years!) The telephone area boundary is different again—halfway between Todmorden and Hebden Bridge. East of that is Bradford; west of it to Todmorden and then south to Manchester, the numbers are in the Manchester North-East directory (with the Manager's Office at Blackburn!). Fortunately (for their sanity) the Pennine folk tend to ignore the boundaries and, since the local government rationalisation, have tended to draw together, recognising their problems as peculiarly their own, needing their own solutions.

The Winter of '79

The Pennines remained and, as if to point up the illogicality of man-made boundaries, continued to strike back in their own way. Their climate is different and undiscriminating. Fog can shroud Manchester, leaving the Pennine Greater Manchester area in clear sunlight. It can be raining at one end of Kirklees and dry at the other. The weather forecasters recognise the anomalies and take care to refer to 'areas over and to the west (or east) of the Pennines'.

The Pennines asserted their authority in the early days of 1979. There had been snow, typically, in November, then a little more just after Christmas. Then a series of gigantic blizzards hit the area and the problems were compounded by a work-to-rule by clearance workers. The winter of '79 added to the store of Pennine legend—for example the story of pavements in Littleborough which had six inches of packed snow on them, the frost so cold that it cracked them like so many biscuits, and that was only in the centre of the town! It was a 'white-out' with fine, powdered snow driven horizontally by a gale-force wind.

Comparisons were inevitably made. 1939–40 was worse (perhaps), 1947 had been much worse, with deeper snow and the ice on Hollingworth Lake over a foot thick, but 1979 produced its own particular agonies. The trans-Pennine roads were blocked, but the motorway, they said, would never close. It did. The valley-road through Littleborough and Todmorden was re-opened and Greater Manchester Police, secure in their city-centre headquarters, advised motorists to leave the motorway at Rochdale and use the Littleborough–Todmorden–Halifax route; so the traffic from eight major trans-Pennine roads plus the motorway tried to squeeze itself through the Summit Pass and Calderdale. The buses were ordered back to the garages—it was simply too dangerous to continue running and the traffic inched its way along the one remaining road open. Soon, the cars and lorries were snowed up on the motorway itself between Rochdale and Heywood, and still the traffic crawled from Rochdale to Todmorden and on to Halifax. It was taking over three hours to travel the 3 miles from Rochdale to Littleborough and, coming in the other direction, a driver had taken seven to cover the 17 miles from Halifax.

Then a lorry skidded and broadsided across the road at Summit. Twenty miles of traffic stopped and would have stayed stopped if it had not been for the local residents. They came out with sacking, cinders—anything that would get the lorry's wheels gripping again. Eventually they succeeded and the traffic ground on again. The stories multiplied as the blizzard raged. Police officers, struggling to find cars buried in the snow over Standedge, had worked roped together. A couple struggling to make their way home to their moorland cottage left their car and struggled, knee-deep, *over the top of a line of garages*. The Lydgate Inn at Littleborough had a wedding reception booked in. There was no hope of the party reaching the inn, so the reception was re-booked at a pub at a lower level and the wedding cake was dragged over 10ft drifts on a sledge. It was to be nearly four months before the snow finally disappeared from the hills.

Lancashire is not Lancashire any more and Yorkshire is split asunder, the Todmorden Joint Omnibus Company has gone forever and the Lancashire & Yorkshire Railway main line is just a minor bit of British Rail and split between two regions. But these changes are in someone else's mind. In their own minds, the people of the Pennines, native and newcomer alike, look from their valley to the hills and across from moor-top to moor-top, trace the ancient track-ways, follow the canals and railways and see what they brought and what they destroyed. The Pennines are always there, softly gleaming or harsh black against a stormy sky, mist-haunted or shattering white against a pale, clear winter sky. The hills have survived a century and a half of grime and gruesome toil and have emerged unscathed, primitively and breathtakingly beautiful. As industry falls away, the country-side creeps back, of its own accord or helped gently on its way by the gardeners and the greenery lovers. The stone buildings, stripped of their sooty coating, glitter in the cleaner air, blur into the mist or lean, seemingly, into the wind.

Probing the shadow-haunted valleys to lift the secrets from the stones, or striding free and wind-danced on the high moor, Pennine people are finding their heritage. What they find is something strangely special and oddly *complete*—an alien thing, but something that is nearer to them in heart and mind than to most other—less fortunate—people.

LIST OF SOURCES

Ashmore, Owen. *Industrial Archaeology of Lancashire* (David & Charles, 1969)

Ashworth, Alan and Parry, Keith. *The Rochdale Then and Now* (Rochdale Canal Society, 1975)

Beautiful Littleborough Society. *Proceedings* (Repub. Littleborough Civic Trust, 1974)

Brett & Gilham. *Great British Tramway Networks* (LRTL, 1962)

Colligan, A. W. *Non-Conformist Chapels in Littleborough* (A. W. Colligan, 1977)

Colligan, A. W. *The Village Church* (Upjohn & Bottomley, 1974)

Collins, Herbert C. *Roof of Lancashire* (J. M. Dent, 1950)

Collins, Herbert C. *South Pennine Park* (Dalesman Books, 1974)

Ellis, David and Fletcher, David. Pennine Park Association— *Report*

Great Manchester MCC. *Strategic Survey* (1979)

Helmshore Local History Society. *Lancashire, the First Industrial Society* (1969)

Hirst, Francis W. *Gordon Harvey* (Richard Cobden-Sanderson, 1925)

Innes, R. *Halifax Piece Hall* (Calderdale MB, 1975)

Johnson, Peter. *M62—The Trans-Pennine Motorway* (Dalesman Books, 1972)

Littleborough Local History Society/Rochdale MB. *History Trails*, 1–5 (1976–9)

Marshall, John. *Lancashire & Yorkshire Railway*, 1/2 (David & Charles, 1969)

Mitchell, Susan. 'Crimsworth Dean', *Pennine Magazine* (Oct/Nov 1979)

Nortcliffe, David. Halifax Town Trail (Calderdale MB, 1979)

North West Water Authority. *South West Pennine Catchment Study* (1978)

Oldham, Kenneth. *The Pennine Way* (Dalesman Books, 1972)

Pennine Development Trust. *Nutclough Mill—Historical Notes* (1979)

Perry, D. *The Rochdale Canal* (Waterways Handbooks Co, 1979)

Round, Philip. *Heptonstall History Trail* (Calder Civic Trust, 1974)

Royal Commission on Canals and Waterways. *Report*, 4 (HMSO, 1908)

Savage, E. M. *Development of Todmorden 1700–1896* (Todmorden Antiquarian Society, 1971)

Waterways Association. *Digest of Report* (1913)

Wheatsheaf. 'How the Food Came to Dublin' (CWS, 1913)

Wrigley, Ammon. *Annals of Saddleworth* (1900, repub. George Kelsall, 1979)

Yorkshire MCC/Countryside Commission. *The Calderdale Way* (1978)

ACKNOWLEDGEMENTS

Photographs are reproduced by permission of the following: The *Halifax Courier* (18); Littleborough Local History Society (9, 13, 15, 16); Metropolitan Borough of Calderdale (8); South Pennine Tourist Information Service (2, 5, 6, 7, 14, 19, 20, cover); West Yorkshire Metropolitan County Council (17).

INDEX

195